IS DEATH FOR REAL?

IS DEATH FOR REAL?

An Examination of Reported Near-Death Experiences in the Light of the Resurrection

Jack W. Provonsha, M.D., Ph.D.

Pacific Press Publishing Association
Mountain View, California
Oshawa, Ontario

Library of Congress Cataloging in Publication Data

Provonsha, Jack W.
Is death for real?
1. Death. 2. Death, Apparent. 3. Future life. 4. Seventh-day Adventists—Doctrinal and controversial works. I. Title.
BT825.P76 236'.1 80-26647
ISBN 0-8163-0406-8

CONTENTS

Do Dead Men Tell Tales?

"About a year ago, I was admitted to the hospital with heart trouble, and the next morning lying in the hospital bed, I began to have a very severe pain in my chest. I pushed the button beside the bed to call for the nurses, and they came in and started working on me. I was quite uncomfortable lying on my back so I turned over, and as I did I quit breathing and my heart stopped beating. Just then, I heard the nurses shout, 'Code pink! Code pink!' As they were saying this I could feel myself moving out of my body and sliding down between the mattress and the rail on the side of the bed—actually it seemed as if I went through the rail—on down to the floor. Then, I started rising upward, slowly. On my way up, I saw more nurses coming running into the room—there must have been a dozen of them. My doctor happened to be making his rounds in the hospital so they called him and I saw him come in, too. I thought, 'I wonder what he's doing here?' I drifted on up past the light fixture—I saw it from the side and very distinctly—and then I stopped, floating right below the ceiling, looking down. I felt almost as though I were a piece of paper that someone had blown up to the ceiling.

"I watched them reviving me from up there! My body was lying down there stretched out on the bed, in plain view, and they were all standing around it. I heard one nurse say, 'Oh my God! She's gone!', while another one leaned down to give me mouth-to-mouth resuscitation. I was looking at the *back* of her head while she did this. I'll never forget the way her hair looked; it was cut kind of short. Just then, I saw them roll this machine in there, and they put the shocks on my chest. When they did, I saw my whole body just jump right up off the bed, and I heard every bone in my body crack and pop. It was the most awful thing!

"As I saw them below beating on my chest and rubbing my arms and legs, I thought, "Why are they going to so much trouble? I'm just fine now.' "[1]

* * * *

"Suddenly she looked eagerly towards one part of the room, a radiant smile illuminating her whole countenance. 'Oh, lovely, lovely,' she said. I asked, 'What is lovely?' 'What I *see*,' she replied in low intense tones. 'What do you see?' 'Lovely brightness—wonderful beings.' It is difficult to describe the sense of reality conveyed by her intense absorption in the vision. Then—seeming to focus her attention more intently on one place for a moment—she exclaimed, almost with a kind of joyous cry, 'Why, it's Father! Oh, he's so glad I'm coming; he *is* so glad. It would be perfect if only W. [her husband] would come too.'

"Her baby was brought to her to see. She looked at it with interest, and then said, 'Do you think I ought to stay for baby's sake?' Then turning towards the vision again, she said, 'I can't—I can't stay, if you could see what I do, you would know I can't stay.' . . . She turned to her husband, who had come in, and said, 'You won't let baby go to anyone who won't love him, will you?' Then she gently pushed him to one side, saying, 'Let me see the lovely brightness.' . . . She spoke to her father, saying 'I am coming. . . . You do want me, Dad; I am coming.' "[2]

What is going on here? For ages dying men and women have looked to the future with mixed feelings of anxiety, uncertainty and even terror. A minority to tough-minded "realists" have faced our brief moment in the sun as an "isthmus between two eternities" of nothingness, but most people in whatever time or place have clung tenaciously to at least the hope that this life was a prelude to something more—and perhaps better.

The fact that men have believed in an afterlife for so long and in so many different cultural settings suggests that the conviction is related to qualities that all of us share as humans. What are these universals in human experience?

First of all is the fact of death itself. Not that all men experience their own deaths, probably most do not, but they do experience the death of others and anticipate their own. It is the ultimate, universal anxiety to which almost all other anxieties relate. In a brilliant, Pulitzer prize-winning book, *The Denial of Death,* Ernest Becker observes: "The idea of death, the fear of it, haunts the human animal like nothing else; it is a mainspring of human activity—activity designed largely to avoid the fatality of death, to overcome it by denying in some way that it is the final destiny for man."[3] As we shall see later, belief in an afterlife may be one of the coping mechanisms by which men have almost universally dealt with their death-fears.

These universals include the difficulty of imagining one's own nonexistence. What child has never wondered what it would feel like to be dead? And of course if death is a descent into nothingness, such wondering is a nonsensical exercise.

Another universal human experience is the difficulty of accepting the death of others. By association-recall the lost ones seem to continue to linger near the places, events, and objects shared with them—even for a long time after they are gone. Gradually new association patterns develop, and the old ones slip away. Some primitives honor their departed as they hover about by ritual worship, their inclusion in festival occasions, etc. The ancient Chinese, for example, seemed undisturbed by the fact that food set out for the departed ancestors appeared to remain uneaten. Since the ancestors were now unseen "spirits," they would naturally eat only the invisible "spiritual" part of the food. Thus do strongly held beliefs create their own legitimation.

All men dream dreams, and dreams easily convey the impression that there is more to a person than just his physical body. While one's body lies at rest on its accustomed pad, another part seems capable of traveling to strange places and doing unusual and interesting things. On awakening this part seems to be reunited again with the body.

Dissociative mystical states can be voluntarily induced by

various yogic exercises, by hypnotic suggestion, by psychedelic drugs, or even by more conventional types of mental illness. These also have always been a part of the shared experience of mankind. All of these in one way or another tend to reinforce the belief that the essence of man lies not in his physical body and that this "something more" may transcend the body in death.

Sometimes individuals experience hallucinations in near-death situations. Herman Melville probably had something like this in mind when he wrote in *Moby Dick*, "For whatever is truly wondrous and fearful in man, never yet was put into words or books. And the drawing near of Death, which alike levels all, alike impresses all with *a last revelation* which only an author from the dead could adequately tell."[4]

But in spite of these shared universals, solid evidence for survival beyond death has been singularly hard to come by. People just did not come back to tell us about it, or at least not often enough to confirm the belief unequivocally. There have always been necromancers, spirit mediums, séances, and the like, purporting to put us in contact with departed souls. But these have been sufficiently interlaced with suggestive, sleight of hand and downright fraud not to be overwhelming, at least to the Harry Houdinis among us.

But now medical technology seems to have changed all that. It is now often possible, we are told, to bring the "departed" back, sometimes to tell us what it was like "on the other side."

Such medical marvels occur with sufficient frequency that it has become difficult even to define death. For example, a patient was brought in by ambulance to the emergency room of a hospital in the eastern part of the United States having suffered a "coronary" while watching his favorite spectator sport. He was conscious, his blood pressure was normal, and he was relatively comfortable from the effects of the shot administered by the nurse at the racetrack. Suddenly his heart stopped. He lost consciousness, and his blood pressure plummeted to zero. To all intents and purposes he had died. The emergency room doctors were equipped to deal with just such contingencies. They took over his breathing with a mechanical ventilator and slammed an electrical charge into his chest.

Gradually his blood pressure returned to normal, and he regained consciousness. A few minutes later he again arrested, and again the sequence was repeated, then again, and again. Twelve times the man "died" in that emergency room, and each time he was revived. He began to say things like, "Well, we got back from that one," "Here we go again." Finally his heart kept beating, and he survived. One physician wondered aloud, "Where was the man's soul during all of this?" A skeptical colleague replied, "It looks like his soul was doing push-ups."

Was the man really dead at any time during that series of crises? By our older criteria, yes. His heart had stopped beating. His blood pressure had fallen to nothing. There was no respiratory movements. His pupils were dilated. These are the vital signs, the absence of which has meant death from times immemorial.

But no more, thanks to modern technology. Death is now seen as a process rather than as a single event. There are several recognized levels of death. The first is brain death, some would say "cortical death," because it can be judged to have happened even while there remains some brainstem activity. ("Personal death" may also be applied to this level.) It is characterized by deep, irreversible coma with no response to stimuli, absence of reflexes, fixed pupils, the need for mechanical assistance for respiration and circulation, and is usually confirmed by flat tracings on the electroencephalograph for a period of twenty-four hours or so. Death statutes are being rewritten so as to conform to this definition.

The older legal, and traditional, definition of death constitutes another level. It involves the disappearance of the obvious vital signs—respiration, heartbeat, blood pressure. This level has been sometimes referred to as "organic death" since it is characterized by the cessation of vital, organ-system activity.

Finally there is cellular death. The cellular structures of the organs in those organ systems continue to live for a variable but relatively brief period after the organ systems themselves have ceased functioning. This period can be extended by cooling the tissues and artificially perfusing them with necessary fluids, oxygen, and nutrients. Cellular death does not occur in all tissues at the same time or at the same rate. The higher centers of the brain suffer irreversible tissue damage early, usually in a relatively few minutes after organ-system death, whereas some tissues remain viable for considerably longer periods.

Cellular death must be prevented if the organs or tissues are to be preserved for transplant purposes. There is often the possibility of reviving the dying subject so long as death has not progressed at this level to more than a minimal degree.

Most of the stories told by persons who have been resuscitated, as in our introductory account,[5] follow a similar general pattern although there is a great deal of variation as to specifics. Not everyone who is resuscitated remembers anything. In fact, most do not. Those who do recall what it was like usually present some variation on the theme of one of Elisabeth Kübler-Ross's patients:

"Mrs. S. had been in and out of the intensive care unit 15 times, never was expected to live, but always made a comeback. In one of her hospitalizations she could not get to Chicago, and she was hospitalized in a local hospital. She remembers being put in a private room, very close to death, and could not make up her mind whether she should call the nurse because she suddenly sensed that she was moments away from death. One part of her wanted very much to lean back in the pillows and finally be at peace. But the other part of her needed to make it through one more time because her youngest son was not yet of age. Before she made the decision to call the nurse and go through this whole rigamarole once more, a nurse apparently walked into her room, took one look at her, and dashed out.

"At that moment, she saw herself floating out of her physical body, floating a few feet above her body. She was very surprised at seeing her corpse in that bed. She made funny remarks about how pale she looked, and then to her utter amazement, described how the resuscitation team dashed into her room. She described in minute details how they worked on her, who was in the room first, who was in last, what they wore, what they said—she even repeated a joke of one of the residents who apparently was very apprehensive and started to joke. In the meantime, while everybody worked very desperately to bring her back to physical life, she floated a few feet above her body and had only one need, one wish—to tell them down there, 'Cool it, relax, take it easy, it's OK.'

"Those are her own words. She could perceive absolutely everything that was going on, but they could not perceive her. And then she gave up on them. She was declared dead, and three and a half hours later she made a comeback and lived for another year and a half."[6]

In Dr. Raymond Moody's book none of the subjects had precisely identical experiences. Commonly they had difficulty finding words to describe what had taken place. Sometimes they heard themselves pronounced dead. Often there were feelings of profound peace and quiet. A soldier in Vietnam later recalled, when he was hit, feeling, "a great attitude of relief. There was no pain, and I've never felt so relaxed. I was at ease and it was all good."[7] Some described unusual auditory sensations, sometimes pleasant, at other times annoying. Frequently references were made to being in a dark space, a tunnel, or a cave. One with a religious background identified this with "the valley of the shadow of death."

Being outside of the body was experienced by most of his subjects. Some of them felt panicky lest they might not be able to get back in again. They reported feelings of weightlessness and an altered sense of time. Almost everyone had a feeling of timelessness. For some, time seemed to stand still. Others felt intense time acceleration. Frequently the senses seemed to be more acute.

Quite a few recounted being aware of other "spiritual beings" in their vicinity who seemed to be there to ease the period of transition. Sometimes these beings were perceived as previously departed friends or loved ones. One of Moody's subjects remembered things this way:

"Several weeks before I nearly died, a good friend of mine, Bob, had been killed. Now the moment I got out of my body I had the feeling that Bob was standing there, right next to me. I could see him in my mind and felt like he was there, but it was strange. I didn't see him as his physical body. I could see things, but not in the physical form, yet just as clearly, his looks, everything. Does that make sense? He was there but he didn't have a physical body. It was kind of like a clear body, and I could sense every part of it—arms, legs, and so on—but I wasn't *seeing* it physically. I didn't think about it being odd at the time because I didn't really need to see him with my eyes. I didn't have eyes, anyway.

"I kept asking him, 'Bob, where do I go now? What has happened? Am I dead or not?' And he never answered me, never said a word. But often, while I was in the hospital, he would be there, and I would ask him again, 'What's going on?', but never any answer. And then the day the doctors said, 'He's going to live,' he left. I didn't see him again and didn't feel his presence. It was almost as though he were waiting until I passed that final frontier and then he would tell me, would give me the details on what was going on."[8]

One said, "I really couldn't say that I talked to any *bodily* people. Yet, I had the feeling that there were people around me, and I could feel their presence, and could feel them moving, though I could never see anyone."[9]

Many of Moody's subjects experienced an encounter with a very bright light. At first dim, the light became increasingly brighter until it reached "unearthly brilliance." All who experienced this had no doubt that it was a personal being emanating love and acceptance. The precise identity of this "being" varied according to the religious presuppositions of the subjects involved—some spoke of an angel, others of Christ. All agreed that they felt total love and acceptance in its presence. Said one subject, "It was beautiful and so bright, so radiant, but it didn't hurt my eyes. It's not any kind of light you can describe on earth. I didn't actually see a person in this light, and yet it has a special identity, it definitely does. It is a light of perfect understanding and perfect love. . . . I felt as though I were surrounded by an overwhelming love and compassion."[10]

It was common for his subjects to recall their past lives in sometimes incredibly rapid, vivid detail; in moving vibrant, three-dimensional color. Often the past was experienced as a series of brilliant flashbacks. Said one, "The whole thing was really odd. I was there; I was actually seeing these flashbacks;

I was actually walking through them, and it was so fast."[11] Said another, "My whole entire life was there at the end of this tunnel, just flashing in front of me. It was not exactly in terms of pictures, more in the form of thought, I guess. I can't exactly describe it to you, but it was just all there. It was just all there at once, I mean, not one thing at a time."[12] Another said, "My whole life kind of flashed in front of me. . . . It was so rapid it was like looking through a volume of my entire life and being able to do it within seconds."[13]

Many reported that the experience had "broadened and deepened" their lives. That it had made them "more reflective and concerned with ultimate philosophical issues." Said one, "The understanding I have of things now is so much better." Said another, "It seems that I am more in tune with people now. . . . I can sense the needs in other individual's lives." According to Moody almost every one of these persons stressed a new feeling of "the importance in this life of trying to cultivate love for others, a love of a unique and profound kind."[14]

Practically all of them came to view death in a new light, without fear. They became convinced that there *is* life after death and came to view death as a release. Interestingly, none of the subjects in Moody's original book experienced the "hereafter" in traditional "mythological" terms. He says, "No one has described the cartoonist's heaven of pearly gates, golden streets, and winged, harp-playing angels, nor a hell of flames and demons with pitchforks."[15] Most rejected the whole reward-punishment model. "They found, much to their amazement, that even when their most apparently awful and sinful deeds were made manifest before the being of light, the being responded not with anger and rage, but rather only with understanding, and even with humor."[16]

Raymond Moody's sequel to *Life After Life*, *Reflections on Life After Life*,[17] adds little to the earlier narratives. There was more of timelessness and "flashes of universal insight,"[18] but now some had heavenly visions reminiscent of what is described in the Bible. There were "cities of light," bright colors, people who had died, flowers, a river "like glass."[19]

Several people reported having glimpsed other beings who seemed trapped in an unfortunate state somewhere between this physical world and "the other side." They seemed unable to surrender their attachments to the physical world. "One man recounted that the spirits he saw apparently 'couldn't progress on the other side because their God is still living here.' "[20] A woman described "bewildered people" in a dull state that contrasted with "all the brilliant light." They seemed sad and depressed and seemed to shuffle as they moved, though she couldn't recall having seen any feet. They were dull, gray, and looked washed out—forever moving but in no particular direction.[21] In several accounts spiritual beings interposed themselves to rescue individuals who were facing death from one cause or another.[22]

In a more recent work, *At the Hour of Death*,[23] parapsychologists Karlis Osis and Erlendur Haraldsson make an apparently serious attempt to apply the methods of scientific, computer analysis to such occurrences. In their study a large number of physicians and nurses were asked to respond to a questionnaire regarding patients they could recall who had had unusual experiences at times when death seemed imminent. They were able to obtain data in this way on over a thousand patients in America and India. (They chose these two different cultures as a way of cross-checking their results.)

Unfortunately, the attempt to bring scientific respectability to their research is marred somewhat by obvious patient and researcher bias. To have made up one's mind about something in advance and then to set out to prove it may make good apologetics, but it usually makes poor science. One is reminded of the counsel of a renowned scientist to his young research assistant, "Beware, young man; you may find what you are looking for." Bias is present in both the selection and in the interpretation of the data, undoubtedly due to the fact that both men are firm believers in life after death. They freely attest to this belief in the way they marshal their supporting evidence.

Their study's chief value lies in the attention it draws to the fact that a certain percentage of persons in impending-death settings (Osis and Haraldsson make only minimal reference to resuscitated patients) will hallucinate even if they are apparently not under obvious, severe stress (one can hardly imagine an impending-death state totally devoid of stress), but are suffering from disease, or are under the influence of drugs commonly associated with hallucinations.

The authors claim to pay little heed to the specific details of the reported hallucinations. They recognize that the almost infinite variety of detail implies that the content is conditioned by the beliefs and expectations of the subjects. Their hypothesis is that the awareness of the "beyond" is a kind of extrasensory perception (ESP) experience more likely to involve mood alteration than having specific ideational content. The commonality of this mood alteration is taken as an indication of a reality to which it corresponds.

One of the unfortunate impressions given by Osis and Haraldsson's book is that these experiences are frequent. A careful reading of their statistics reveals this not to be the case. Most persons in such situations do not experience hallucinations of this sort, or of any other for that matter. One study indicates that the figure is about 10 percent.[24,25]

At the Hour of Death makes much of the common core of these experiences, cross-culturally as well as from individual to individual. The implication is that this common core confirms the reality to which it seems to point. In their eagerness to confirm their hypothesis, however, the authors pay insufficient attention to other possible sources of this commonality including factors derived from the fact of shared humanness. Moreover, there is a greater cross-cultural commonness underlying religious belief than they seem to recognize. The two cultures they studied, for example, share a great deal more than is readily observed.

Osis and Haraldsson's argument for the existence of the reality of life after death based on the common-core quality of these experiences is reminiscent of the historical argument for the existence of God. That argument notes the fact that all men everywhere worship. This observation confirms the existence of the central object(s) of worship since it must have a cause. Unfortunately, as we know, there could be other causes. Sigmund Freud reminded us that all men everywhere have also had parents. It was this fact, he believed, that was the basis for what he called the "illusion" of a cosmic father. In these near-death experiences also we must be prepared to encounter possible explanations. We shall now look at some of them.

References

1. Raymond A. Moody, Jr., *Life After Life* (Covington, Georgia: Bantam Book, Mockingbird Books, 1976), pp. 35, 36. Quoted material from *Life After Life* on this and subsequent pages is used by permission of the copyright owners, Mockingbird Books, St. Simons Island, Georgia.

2. Karlis Osis and Erlendur Haraldsson, *At the Hour of Death* (New York: Avon Books, 1977), pp. 15, 16.

3. Ernest Becker, *The Denial of Death* (New York: The Free Press, 1973), p. ix.

4. Herman Melville, *Moby Dick* (New York: Hendricks House, 1952), p. 473. (Emphasis supplied.)

5. Dr. Moody entitled his book *Life After Life* rather than *Life After Death* and referred to "near-death" throughout his book, because as a physician he knew that none of his resuscitated subjects qualified for death by the updated criteria. In every case the condition was at least temporarily reversible. If they had truly died, resuscitation would not have been possible. Medical science with all of its wonders is still a long way from doing resurrections!

6. Elisabeth Kübler-Ross, "Death Does Not Exist," *The Journal of Holistic Health*, 1977, pp. 62, 63.

7. Moody, *Life After Life*, p. 29.

8. *Ibid.*, p. 56.

9. *Ibid.*, p. 58.

10. *Ibid.*, p. 63.

11. *Ibid.*, p. 68.

12. *Ibid.*, p. 69.

13. *Ibid.*, pp. 69, 70.

14. *Ibid.*, p. 92.

15. *Ibid.*, p. 97.

16. *Ibid.*, pp. 97, 98.

17. Raymond Moody, *Reflections on Life After Life* (New York: Bantam Books, 1978).

18. *Ibid.*, p. 10.

19. *Ibid.*, pp. 17, 18.

20. *Ibid.*, p. 18.

21. *Ibid.*, p. 19.

22. *Ibid.*, p. 23ff.

23. Karlis and Haraldsson, *At the Hour of Death*.

24. Ian Stevensen, "Research into the Evidence of Man's Survival After Death," *The Journal of Nervous and Mental Disease* 165, no. 3 (1977): 155.

25. Abraham Maslow speaks of "peakers," a small percentage of the general population, who while mainly like everyone else, may experience, on occasion, spontaneous, mystical states. Are the persons in Osis and Haraldsson's study also ordinarily natural "peakers"? They say nothing about this. They do refer to the similarities of these impending-death experiences to

those of the classical mystics. And in many ways the similarities are clear and obvious. Have Osis and Haraldsson unintentionally selected out a group of peakers—or potential peakers who, placed in an impending-death setting, or at least the unusual setting of a hospital, are momentarily being mystically "turned on"?

Dreams, Drugs, and Death Visions

To keep perspective it should be noted that in a number of other circumstances similar experiences occur. One of the patients at Loma Linda University Medical Center reported that at least fifteen times over a ten-year period he had "left" his body. Each time he hovered just above his body struggling to maintain contact with it. He was afraid that he might not be able to get back into his body. The patient was eventually diagnosed as having a slow-growing pituitary tumor which was surgically removed. His only clinical abnormality was an elevated serum prolactin level. This condition sometimes indicates a hormone-producing pituitary tumor. Except for the recurrent episodes of leaving his body the patient felt normal. And the phenomenon apparently has ceased since surgery.

Another patient at the same institution, a nurse, could have been a candidate for Dr. Moody's book. She experienced, while under anesthesia, many of the things described by his subjects.

One of my own patients once told me that while being administered nitrous oxide he had felt his soul leaving his body through the top of his head. Interestingly, those few of Dr. Moody's patients who recalled returning to their bodies often referred to their heads as the "point of reentry."

Osis and Haraldsson purposely selected their cases so as to eliminate obvious causes of hallucinations such as drugs, uremia, and brain injury or disease. Theirs were mainly hospitalized patients who, while not necessarily terminal, were in a setting where death was easily, at least subliminally, suggested. They were generally not patients who had been resuscitated. It is not possible, of course, to eliminate the effects of stress hormones on patients in such a setting, and it is known that stress situations produce chemical changes in the central nervous system.

The most fascinating parallels to Moody's and Kübler-Ross's accounts are found in the so-called psychedelic literature. While often interpreted differently, almost every aspect of the experience described by their subjects is matched line for line by the users of hallucinogens such as LSD.

Such substances produce illusions that are exceedingly variable as to content (as were those of the subjects in *Life After Life*). In part this is thought to be due to the high level of suggestability that is characteristic of dissociative states. Environmental cues, conceptual presuppositions, belief systems, and expectations have enormous power to shape such states. There are some features that are present often enough, however, to be considered coreconstants. And these appear at least as frequently in the drugged state as in Moody's *Life After Life* accounts.

One is ineffability or indescribability. The drugged state seemed "beyond words" as frequently as did the state of the "afterlife," although both groups often tried desperately to describe it.

Another is the illusion of being "out of the body." Timothy Leary related an experience he had after eating certain mushrooms (*Psilocybe mexicana*) he had purchased from a mountain crone called Crazy Juana, on a visit to Cuernavaca, Mexico. "I realized I had died, that I Timothy Leary, the Timothy Leary game, was gone. I could look back and see my body on the bed. I relived my life, and re-experienced many events I had forgotten."[1]

One of Sanford Unger's subjects on LSD said, "My ideas of space were strange beyond description. I could see myself from head to foot as well as the sofa on which I was lying. About me was nothingness, absolutely empty space. I was floating on a solitary island in the ether. No part of my body was subject to the laws of gravitation."[2]

Subjects frequently report such feelings as the following: "My body is no longer my own." "I feel like a bystander watching myself." "I feel as if I have no body." One described his experience this way: "I feel as though my body is melting away; I have no boundaries—scoop me up off the floor and tie me in a sack to give me some limits." Later he said, "I feel like I'm blended with the universe."[3]

Aldous Huxley said after taking mescaline, "My body seemed to have dissociated itself almost completely from my mind. . . . My awareness of the transfigured outer world was no longer accompanied by an awareness of my physical organism. . . . It was odd, of course, to feel that 'I' was not the same as these arms and legs 'out there,' as this wholly objective trunk and neck and even head. It was odd; but one soon got used to it. And anyhow the body seemed perfectly able to look after itself."[4]

Frosch writes of a twenty-one-year-old woman who was admitted to the hospital along with her lover: "She became frightened when she realized that she was unable to distinguish her body from the chair she was sitting on or from her lover's body. Her fear became more marked after she thought she would not get back into herself."[5]

It was this feeling of dissociation from the body that formed the basis for a number of therapeutic experiments on the treatment of terminally ill patients. In Kast and Collin's series, patients on LSD came to view their serious conditions with a peculiar disregard. They were able to speak more freely about what lay before them and with less depression. They also developed a greater sense of community with their fellow patients. Some interpreted their "transcendental" reactions to the drug in terms of survival after death.[6]

Jane Dunlap's husband suggested after an LSD experience that "LSD should be given to all persons suffering terminal illness; not only would their agonies be hushed, but their passing could be an event of great happiness."[7] One of Sidney Cohen's terminal cancer patients said while on LSD, "My extinction is not of great consequence at this moment, not even for me. . . . I suppose that I'm detached—that's it—away from myself and my pain and my decaying." Said another, "Ah, yes,

I see what you have done. You have stripped away ME. This is a touch of death—a preparation for the big one when the No-Me will be more permanent."[8]

Mary Barnard thinks that such substances, even perhaps accidently ingested as hallucinogenic plants, may have been a major source of belief in the afterlife, because the conviction of independency from the body they instill is so strong.[9]

Said one subject while on LSD, "I was immediately aware that I exist . . . always . . . in a transphysical universe, . . . that the 'I' I was now experiencing had existed long before the physical me was born and would continue to exist long after that organism was dead . . . outside of physical time and space."[10]

To Jane Dunlap, "what had heretofore been merely an intellectual concept thus became an emotionally charged conviction: that our souls, the God part of ourselves, would live throughout all eternity, remaining forever deathless."[11]

One of the striking similarities among Moody's subjects, those of Osis and Haraldsson, and individuals who have been exposed to these powerful psychochemicals is the attitudinal changes afterward—toward themselves, toward others, and toward life in general. They frequently reported feelings of having solved the riddle of existence. John Blofield said after taking mescaline, "I felt as though, after many years of anxious search for the answer to some momentous problem, I was suddenly confronted with the solution so wholly satisfying that I had to burst out laughing. I was conscious of immense joy."[12]

Korngold described his LSD experience in terms reminiscent of individuals undergoing sudden religious conversion. It carried "the quality of surprise, of wonder, of revelation, of pristine perceptual innocence, as if seeing something with brand new eyes."[13] Aldous Huxley spoke of "looking at a new creation."[14] Timothy Leary wrote of profound feelings of "seeing things as they are."[15]

Expressions like "being reborn" and "new birth" appear frequently in the psychedelic literature. Sherwood states that a single experience under LSD can be so impressive as to change one's life for months and years afterward.[16] These changes are reported as subjective feelings of well-being, inner strength, and confidence;[17] of increased self-understanding and understanding of others;[18] of a decrease in rigidity;[19] and of a state of relaxation and freedom from irritability.[20]

More than half of one group of individuals who had taken LSD claimed that they had had "the deepest spiritual experience of their life."[21] Many users reported "a greater awareness of God, or a higher power, or Ultimate Reality," "greater tolerance of others," and "a set of new decisions and new directions for . . . life."[22]

An increased ability to have faith and trust in others is frequently reported as a consequence of seeing oneself in a different light.[23]

Leary described a feeling of intense love dominating the state.[24]

After mescaline John Blofield said, "A single glimpse of what I saw should be enough to call forth unbounded affection for all living beings: . . . however ugly, smelly, or tiresome they may seem, . . . hatred, dislike, disdain, aversion for any being . . . must amount to blasphemy in one who has seen Being itself."[25]

According to Richard Blum a large proportion of regular users of LSD report moving from "being dissatisfied with self to being satisfied with self, from feeling unfulfilled to feeling fulfilled, from feeling empty to feeling vital, from having too much to do to having a reasonable amount to do, from having no sense of self-guidance to having control of one's destiny, from being angry to being no longer angry, and from not being loving to being loving. . . . Most regulars had felt unloving before, but all of them now felt that they are loving people."[26]

Jane Dunlap reports a conversation with a friend who had taken several LSD "trips." "I opened the subject immediately by remarking, 'I'm dying to hear what happened.'

" 'I've been dying to tell you, but there's one little fly in the ointment. It's untellable.'

"I had no idea what she meant, but her high color, quick breathing, and the expression of her face showed she was overcome with emotion.

" 'What did you see?' I persisted.

" 'I saw God.'

" 'But what was it you actually saw?'

" 'I really didn't see anything, but I felt His presence. It was so overpowering it forced you to love everyone. In fact, it was impossible not to love everyone, even for weeks afterward.' "[27]

There are a number of other, somewhat incidental, similarities between the drug and the near-death experiences appearing only infrequently. These include a radically altered time sense, perceptual sensitivity, heightened awareness, lights, tunnels, caverns, and darkness.

Another interesting parallel involves the effects of carbon dioxide. Carbon dioxide administration differs from the usual psychedelics to some extent but produces many similar effects. L. J. Meduna analyzed responses to the administration of thirty-percent carbon dioxide on a large number of subjects and summed these up with the statement, "We definitely can see that the form-constants in Mescal [mescaline] vision . . . are present in the sensory alterations produced by CO_2."[28]

The following reports by subjects on carbon dioxide are typical: "I felt as though I was looking down at myself, as though I was way out here in space. . . . I felt sort of separated."[29] "There was a large audience in an amphitheatre or something and I just floated whirling above the audience."[30]

Following an initial experience of brilliant colors and designs one subject reported, "I felt myself being separated; my soul, drawing apart from the physical being, was drawn upward seemingly to leave the earth and to go upward where it reached a greater Spirit with whom there was a communion, producing a remarkable, new relaxation and deep security. Through this communion I seemed to receive assurance that the petit problems or whatever was bothering the human being that was me huddled down on earth, would work out all right and that I had no need to worry.

"In this spirituelle I felt the Greater Spirit even smiling indulgently upon me in my vain little efforts to carry on by myself and I pressed close the warmth and tender strength and felt assurance of enough power to overcome whatever lay ahead for me as a human being."[31]

Said another, "I had an impression of being in complete understanding and harmony with God. Seemed like an abrupt awakening of truths I should have known but somehow hadn't known before. Failures and successes faded into insignificance and I was part of an all-consuming *love*—so strong and intense and beautiful—everything was right."[32]

Again, as with the drugs and near-death, there were reports of caves, tunnels, visions of other persons, luminaries, reliving of the past, etc. One described "a white spot in the center of a dark field. The spot had begun to grow and become lighter and lighter until he felt as if he were looking into the glaring sun."[33] Interestingly, the eye with which this light was seen had been blind since the age of three. Elisabeth Kübler-Ross says that her subjects' "spiritual forms" are complete, functional, and unimpaired when "out of the body"—even though the bodies they left might actually have had such defects as blindness and missing limbs.

Raymond Moody's and Elisabeth Kübler-Ross's subjects were undoubtedly not on hallucinogenic drugs, and neither were those of Osis and Haraldsson by selective design. But the point is that altered central-nervous-system chemistry *can* produce similar illusions and hallucinations. Recall that the content of those illusions and hallucinations differed widely according to variations in belief systems, expectations, and environmental cues. These chemical alterations may be produced by extrinsic agents such as the psychedelic drugs, but they may also be brought about by internal, biochemical factors as is suggested by the carbon dioxide data.

During the dying process, when there is organ-system suspension as in cardiac arrest, fairly profound modifications would take place at the level of cellular metabolism—including the buildup of carbon dioxide due to the failure of circulation. This might be a relatively limited factor in the brain because of its peculiar metabolism, but carbon dioxide accumulation along with other metabolites could well be sufficient to produce the observed effects. It is of some interest that the kind of experiences Raymond Moody describes occur only when cardiac arrest is gradual—allowing time for the metabolites to accumulate. They do not occur when the heart stops suddenly as in Stokes-Adams attack.[34]

Much remains unknown about the biochemical changes

which occur during dying, including the role of endorphins, but the above remains a viable alternative to the interpretation of these experiences presently given by the authors to whom we have referred. It could just be that such experiences as those referred to in *Life After Life* represent the later recall of psychochemically induced hallucinations and illusions brought on by the physiologic dying process—conditioned by belief systems, expectations, and environmental cues. Psychotrophic chemicals such as the hallucinogens, carbon dioxide, and anesthetic agents (and perhaps such things as elevated prolactin levels) *can* produce analogous phenomena. This fact renders this explanation at least plausible. Psychological factors, including the effects of stress hormones in possible-death situations, may be more subtle but nonetheless important once we have sorted them out.

Some of the features of life-after-death phenomena, however, may not be so easily explained. An example is the reappearance of Elisabeth Kübler-Ross's Mrs. S. some months after her death and burial.

Dr. Kübler-Ross gives an account. It was a strange and unsettling encounter, causing Dr. Kübler-Ross to wonder, as a psychiatrist, about her own sanity. The apparition came, she said, to urge her not to give up her work on death and dying. (Dr. Kübler-Ross had been contemplating discontinuing her seminar on the topic.) She also wanted Dr. Kübler-Ross to convey her thanks to a former colleague for his help. Wanting some scientific evidence of the visit Dr. Kübler-Ross asked the visitor for a written note that she could keep. She was obliged, and she still retains this note as a memento of the occasion.

What to make of this account? Was Dr. Kübler-Ross experiencing one of Osis and Haraldsson's apparition hallucinations? She certainly was not in any impending-death situation. Moreover, no hallucinations that we know of ever write notes to be framed under glass. Was she involved in a delusional system in which the woman was really someone other than Dr. Kübler-Ross's Mrs. S., though believed by her to be her former patient? (Recall her uncertainty at the outset and her difficulty in remembering the woman's name. Handwriting comparisons might be useful. Dr. Kübler-Ross doesn't mention having done that.) We probably will never know. But the experience apparently left little doubt in Dr. Elisabeth Kübler-Ross's mind about the personal survival of the dead. Later she was given information by "spirit entities" that her work with dying patients was finished, "that there are many people who can carry on now, that this was not my real job, why I'm on the earth. . . . The whole work with death and dying was simply a testing ground for me. . . . My real job is . . . to tell people that death does not exist."[35]

Elisabeth Kübler-Ross's recent involvement with spiritual "entities" and some fairly this-worldly human advisors in southern California—along with charges of sexual misconduct, including the alleged molestation of a ten-year-old girl by supposed "spirit entities" (the whole thing makes for rather lurid reading)—raises considerable question as to whether she should now be taken seriously. Some of her former colleagues apparently now do not.[36]

Osis and Haraldsson selected their subjects mainly from individuals who had experienced hallucinations supporting belief in an afterlife near the time of death but were otherwise unimpaired—that is, there was no apparent brain disease or injury, uremic poisoning, or the like. Mainly these consisted of visual hallucinations of persons, frequently previously departed, who came to get them; of "heavenly" places, and of mood changes—often persisting as a more relaxed and peaceful attitude. This contrasts with Moody's preoccupation with the recall of individuals who had been resuscitated from near-death—usually following cardiac arrest and the disappearance of the traditional vital signs.

Russell Noyes, Jr., M.D. (associate professor of psychiatry, University of Iowa College of Medicine) and Roy Kletti, M.A. (clinical psychologist at the same institution) approached subjects in similar situations but with quite different interest and presuppositions. Neither states a belief in the afterlife nor is apparently interested in finding support for it. It is apparent that they think it is possible to account for these experiences on purely psychological terms. Dr. Noyes frankly states his intention of offering a psychodynamic interpretation which "may provide a framework for understanding and interpreting a final stage in the dying process," with the hope that this "may point to ways of manipulating it to advantage."[37]

Dr. Noyes's examples are mainly drawn from individuals who face the imminent prospect of death from falling from cliffs, from anaphylaxis (severe shock reaction to a drug), etc. His cases express all of the features contained in the anecdotes of Kübler-Ross, Moody, and Osis and Haraldsson: the visual hallucinations, the rapid life reviews, the feelings of ineffability, the transcendence, the euphoria—features that are so characteristic of mystical experiences. The only difference is that the interpretation of these experiences comes from a different vantage point—that of objective, psychodynamic analysis.

The work of Noyes and Kletti is laced with psychological jargon such as *regression* and *denial*. To illustrate, the sudden life review is thought of as an attempt by the seriously threatened ego to defend itself by thrusting the past into full consciousness. Since the self is inextricably bound up with past experiences—"I am what I have been"—this represents a desperate ego-saving attempt in the face of imminent loss, a kind of death denial. (Presumably, those interested in more physiologic explanations of mental events would speak of the flooding of the psyche with hallucinogenic stress chemicals stimulated by the stark terror of the situation.)

As support for this kind of psychodynamic interpretation they refer to a study of David H. Rosen of San Francisco in which survivors of suicide leaps from San Francisco Bay bridges never report life review experiences although they share in a number of respects other features of encounters with near-death. This difference is ascribed to the fact that such persons have given up on themselves, and there is therefore no necessity for ego defense. (Unfortunately, Dr. Rosen's series is quite small. Only about 1 percent of such attempts fail.)[38] Heim had reported that 95 percent of his thirty survivors of mountain-climbing falls experienced a sudden review of their past histories.[39]

Noyes and Kletti conclude their joint paper saying, "From our examination of near-death experiences we may conclude that what Heim (1892) wrote over eighty years ago was substantially correct. He described a syndrome commonly reported by emotionally disturbed patients to which the term depersonalization was later applied. The differences between the subjective experiences of individuals in the midst of life-threatening danger and depersonalization among patients may add to our understanding of *this curious disorder*."[40]

The work of Noyes and Kletti forms a useful contrast to that of the other authors we have mentioned. They have examined identical phenomena but found in them in no impelling evidence for a real window on the hereafter.

A similar conclusion is reached by James E. Alcock, professor of psychology at Glendon College, York University, Toronto:

"Each and all of the various characteristics of the 'death' experiences have been found to occur, alone or in a combination, in various 'normal,' non-death circumstances, such as those associated with emotional or physical stress, sensory deprivation, hypnagogic sleep, drug-induced hallucination, and so on. We know that the nervous system can process these experiences, even if we can't always predict when the experiences will occur. . . .

"It is clear that the 'scientific,' 'objective' evidence for life after death is very unimpressive indeed. . . . Survival research is based on belief in search of data rather than observation in search of explanation. It is an extension of individual and collective anxiety about death."[41]

The question before us is, Which point of view is the correct one? Do these near-death experiences give us a fascinating glimpse into a reality beyond this ordinary life, or do they represent "a curious disorder" sometimes encountered in persons in life-threatening situations? How can we determine the truth?

References

1. John Kobler, "The Dangerous Magic of LSD," *Saturday Evening Post* 236 (2 Nov. 1963):31, 32.

2. Sanford M. Unger, "Mescaline, LSD, Psilocybin and Personality Change," *Psychiatry* 26 (May 1963):113 (footnotes).

3. G. D. Klee, "Lysergic Acid Diethylamide (LSD-25) and Ego Function," *Archives of General Psychiatry* 8 (May 1963):463.

4. Aldous Huxley, *The Doors of Perception* (New York: Harper and Brothers, 1956), p. 52.

5. William A. Frosch et al., "Untoward Reactions to Lysergic Acid Diethylamide (LSD) Resulting in Hospitalization," *New England Journal of Medicine* 273 (2 December 1965):1236.

6. E. C. Kast et al., "Study of Lysergic Acid Diethylamide as Analgesic Agent," *Journal of International Anesthetic Research Society* 43 (1964):285-291.

7. Jane Dunlap, *Exploring Inner Space* (New York: Harcourt, Brace and World, 1961), p. 63.

8. Sidney Cohen, "LSD and the Anguish of Dying," Harper's 231 (September 1965):69, 72.

9. Cited in Huston Smith, "Do Drugs Have Religious Import?" in *LSD: The Consciousness Expanding Drug*, ed. David Solomon (New York: G. P. Putnam's Sons, 1964), p. 154.

10. Willis Harman, "The Issue of the Consciousness-expanding Drugs," *Main Currents in Modern Thought* 20 (September-October 1963):11.

11. Dunlap, *Exploring Inner Space*, p. 48.

12. John Blofield, "A High Yogic Experience Achieved With Mescaline," *The Psychedelic Review* no. 7 (1966):11, 12.

13. M. Korngold, "LSD and the Creative Experience," *Psychoanalytic Review* 50 (Winter 1953):684.

14. Aldous Huxley, *Heaven and Hell* (New York: Harper and Brothers, 1956), p. 15.

15. Timothy Leary, "The Religious Experience: It's Production and Interpretation," *The Psychedelic Review* no. 1 (1964):341.

16. J. N. Sherwood et al., "The Psychedelic Experience—A New Concept in Psychotherapy, *Journal of Neuropsychiatry* 8 (November-December 1962):69.

17. Charles Savage et al., *Process and Outcome Variables in Psychedelic (LSD) Therapy* (Menlo Park, Calif.: International Foundation for Advanced Study, n.d.), p. 9.

18. Joseph Havens, "A Working Paper: Memo on the Religious Implications of the Consciousness Changing Drugs," *Journal for the Scientific Study of Religion* 3 (Spring 1964):219.

19. James Terrill, "The Nature of the LSD Experience," in *LSD: The Consciousness-Expanding Drug*, ed. David Solomon (New York: G. P. Putnam's Sons, 1964), p. 179.

20. A. Hoffer, "Studies With Niacin and LSD," in *Lysergic Acid Diethylamide and Mescaline in Experimental Psychiatry*, ed. Louis Cholden (New York: Grune and Stratton, 1956), p. 211.

21. Timothy Leary, "The Religious Experience: Its Production and Interpretation," *The Psychedelic Review* 1 (1964):325.

22. "Editorial," *The Psychedelic Review* 1 (1964):21-23.

23. Joseph J. Downing et al., "Psychedelic Experience and Religious Belief," in *Utopiates: The Use and Users of LSD 25*, ed. Richard Blum et al. (New York: Atherton Press), pp. 164, 169.

24. Timothy Leary et al., *The Psychedelic Experience*, (New York: University Books, 1964), p. 58.

25. Blofield, "A High Yogic Experience," p. 32.

26. Richard Blum et al., "LSD 'Regulars': Continuing Users Compared With Discontinuers," in *Utopiates: The Use and Users of LSD 25,* ed. Richard Blum et al. (New York: Atherton Press, 1964), p. 78.

27. Jane Dunlap, *Exploring Inner Space* (New York: Harcourt, Brace and World, Inc., 1961), pp. 167, 168.

28. L. J. Meduna, ed., *Carbon Dioxide Therapy* (Springfield, Ill.: Charles C. Thomas, 1958), p. 50.

29. *Ibid.*, p. 42.

30. *Ibid.*, p. 41.

31. *Ibid.*, p. 47.

32. *Ibid.*, p. 48.

33. *Ibid.*, p. 63.

34. Richard S. Blacher, "To Sleep, Perchance to Dream . . . " *Journal of the American Medical Association* 242, no. 21 (23 November 1979):2291.

35. Elisabeth Kübler-Ross, "Death Does Not Exist," *The Journal of Holistic Health,* 1977, pp. 64, 65.

36. See Kate Coleman, "Elisabeth Kübler-Ross in the Afterworld of Entities: There's something, well, worldly about her spirit counselors," *New West,* 30 July 1979, pp. 43-50 and *Time,* 12 November 1979, p. 81.

37. Russell Noyes, Jr., "The Experience of Dying," *Psychiatry* 35 (May 1972):174.

38. David H. Rosen, "Suicide Survivors—A Followup Study of Persons Who Survived Jumping From the Golden Gate and San Francisco-Oakland Bay Bridges, *Western Journal of Medicine* 122 (April 1975):289-294.

39. Noyes, "The Experience of Dying," p. 176.

40. Russell Noyes, Jr. and Roy Kletti, "Depersonalization in the Face of Life-Threatening Danger: A Description," *Psychiatry* 39 (February 1976):26, 27. (Emphasis supplied.)

41. James E. Alcock, "Psychology and Near-Death Experiences," *The Skeptical Inquirer,* Spring 1979, pp. 39, 40.

Alcock likens Moody's arguments to an old Abbot and Costello routine, where one of them proves that the other "isn't here": "Are you in London?" "No." "Are you in Paris?" "No." "Are you in Moscow?" "No." "Well, if you aren't in London, Paris, or Moscow, you must be somewhere else." "Yah, I guess so." "Well, if you're somewhere else, you can't be here." *Ibid.*, p. 28.

What Is Man?

The main difficulty in deciding whether these near-death experiences express contact with a higher reality or reflect something much more mundane is that they are private. Private experiences are notoriously difficult to test, at least scientifically.

About all that can be said here for sure is that apparently under certain conditions some people will occasionally have private, mystical experiences which they take "for real." They may even respond to the experience *as if* they were "for real." But since these experiences cannot be laid out on the table for the rest of us to share (as science does in its laboratories), they can neither be confirmed nor disconfirmed in the sense that the word *test* suggests (Osis and Haraldsson's effort notwithstanding).

This does not mean that they do not represent reality. It is just that in terms of the scientific model we cannot know for sure. Such claims must be examined in other ways, for example, by determining whether they are consistent with already established truths or concepts.

Consider how we might go about this in a traditional Christian context. If the Bible is accepted as the normative Word of God (however that acceptance may have been established), any scientifically unverifiable experience can be judged to express reality depending more or less on the extent to which it harmonizes with the Bible's teaching.

The Bible itself suggests such a testing method. The language of the King James Version is quaint but quite clear. "And when they shall say unto you, Seek unto them that have familiar spirits, and unto wizards that peep, and mutter: should not a people seek unto their God? for the living to the dead? To the law and to the testimony [that is, the normative Word]: if they speak not according to this word, it is because there is no light in them." Isaiah 8:19, 20.

People who take the Bible seriously as the Word of God (if not necessarily the very words of God) and who do not build their faith on wish fulfillment, even on death-denial wish fulfillment, or a psychological need should be interested in developments taking place in biblical scholarship over the past half-century. These developments represent a rediscovery, in a way, of a long-lost perspective that has great relevance to the subject at hand.

Elisabeth Kübler-Ross speaks of having collected cases from all over the world, "hundreds of cases from Australia to California" all sharing the same common denominator:

"They all are fully aware of shedding their physical body. And death, as we understood it in scientific language, does really not exist. Death is simply a shedding of the physical body like the butterfly coming out of a cocoon. It is a transition into a higher state of consciousness, where you continue to perceive, to understand, to laugh, to be able to grow, and the only thing that you lose is something you don't need anymore, and that is your physical body. It's like putting away your winter coat when spring comes and you know that the coat is too shabby and you don't want to wear it anymore. That's virtually what death is all about."[1]

When Dr. Kübler-Ross says this, she is conditioned by a conceptual tradition with a long history. The notion entered Christian teachings during centuries of syncretism of Christian, Greco-Roman, and Hebraic ideas.

Its philosophic roots are in what has been called Platonic dualism, not that Plato originated the notion. It was present in Greek thought and literature at least as far back as the sixth century B.C. where belief in the immortality of man's soul clearly appears in the Orphic religion and in the religion of the so-called mysteries.[2]

Plato was no Orphic, of course;[3] and as always ideas are never immaculately conceived. Plato's dualism also had its past. But because he has left us the clearest and most impressive expression of the idea, Plato largely receives the credit.

Let us listen to him in *Phaedo*. Socrates, who is prepared to drink the lethal hemlock, is conversing with his disciples who are anguished at his imminent departure. He is trying to reassure them.

"Well then," added Socrates, "let us suppose that there are two sorts of existences—one seen, the other unseen."

[Cebes] "Let us suppose them."

"The seen is the changing, and the unseen is the unchanging?"

"That may be also supposed."

"And further, is not one part of us body, another part soul?"

"To be sure."

"And to which class is the body more alike and akin?"

"Clearly to the seen—no one can doubt that."

"And is the soul seen or not seen?"

"Not by man, Socrates."

"That soul, I say, herself invisible, departs to the invisible world—to the divine and immortal and rational: thither arriving, she is secure of bliss and is released from the error and folly of men, their fears and wild passions and all other human ills, and forever dwells, as they say of the initiated, in company with the gods. Is not this true, Cebes?"[4]

Again,

"Seeing then that the immortal is indestructible, must not the soul, if she is immortal, be also imperishable?"

"Most certainly."

"Then when death attacks a man, the mortal portion of him may be supposed to die, but the immortal retires at the approach of death and is preserved safe and sound?"

"True."

"Then, Cebes, beyond question, the soul is immortal and imperishable, and our souls will truly exist in another world!"[5]

Later Crito is concerned about the burial of Socrates.

"We shall try our best to do as you say," said Crito, "but how shall we bury you?"

"Any way you like," replied Socrates, "that is, if you can catch me and I don't slip through your fingers." He laughed gently as he spoke, and turning to us went on: "I cannot persuade Crito that I am this Socrates who is here talking to you . . . ; he thinks that I am the one whom he will see presently lying dead. . . . You must give assurance to Crito for me . . . that when I am dead I shall not stay but depart and be gone. That will help Crito to bear more easily . . . when he sees my body being burned or buried, as if something dreadful were happening to me. . . . No, you must keep up your spirits and say that it is only my body that you are burying; and you can bury it as you please."[6]

Such was a major view of man during the early centuries of our era as Christianity moved away from its seeding place in Palestine to take root in the soil of Asia Minor and around the Mediterranean basin. It was almost inevitable that non-Hebrew Christians would bring some of their conceptual presuppositions to their newfound faith.

But their presuppositions, by this time, were not merely those of Plato of a half-millennium before. In the intervening period several things happened to Plato's dualism of soul and body. One of the things that happened was gnosticism and later Manichaeism—both with negative value-feelings about matter in general and bodies in particular. For both, soul existence was the ideal state, and for both the body was not only the temporary house it was for Plato. (Plato appreciated his body even though he thought of it as mortal and changeable.) For these revised Platonists the body was a veritable burden to the soul—inherently evil, to be kept under control and denied for the sake of the soul.

The transition was not immediate, and important modifications of even gnosticized Platonic thought took place as it passed through the hands of the early Christian Fathers, but it was almost inevitable that such a blending of ideas would occur in a world that not only spoke the literal language of Plato but much of the spiritual language as well.

Probably the most important influence in this blending was

the fact that one of the Fathers of Christian theology, Origen of Alexandria, was a Platonic philosopher. Origen simply incorporated Plato's cosmic drama of the soul into his theology. And while some of his later successors thought he incorporated too much, they retained the essence of his Platonic concept of the soul.[7]

Some of the Fathers knew that Plato's conception of immortality was not precisely that of the Scriptures. For Plato the soul was immortal by nature. Most of the Fathers, e.g., Irenaeus, Tatian, Theophilus, Arnobius, Lactantius, and others, maintained the biblical sense of the soul's dependence upon God. Justin Martyr was one of the first to discuss the problem. "It lives not as being itself life," he wrote "but as the partaker of life." This because "God wills it to live, and hence it will cease to live whenever he may please that it shall live no longer, for it is not the property of the soul to have life in itself as it is the property of God."[8] But the fact of the soul's *immortality*, dependent or not, was not itself questioned.

This represents a striking departure from the thought of the Bible. As Werner Jaeger puts it, "The Hebrew Bible does not know immortality in this sense at all, and the idea of resurrection in the New Testament is quite different."[9]

That "interesting development" among Christian theologians of the past half century is the discovery that the underlying concept of man in the Bible differs markedly from the Platonic model, and the difference is sufficiently great to render the two conceptually incompatible.

Part of the problem faced by the earlier theologians lay in the difficulty experienced in capturing the thought forms that lay behind those interesting Hebrew and Greek words that are translated "soul" and "spirit" in our English Bibles.

The Hebrew word for *soul* in the Old Testament is *nephesh*. It appears in the Old Testament a total of 755 times. Usually the translators (remember, by the time they were at work, the Platonic presupposition was well ensconced in Christian anthropology) simply translated *nephesh* as "soul." They recognized from the context that *nephesh* was not precisely the same as what they had come to think of as a "soul." Therefore, in 119 places in the King James Version they translated *nephesh* as "life"; and there are other instances where "life" would have been a better rendering. The word in the Old Testament suggests uniqueness or individuality. Man became a living "soul." Genesis 2:7. (Notice *became,* not received.) Frequently, the term thus means "person" or "individual" as in Genesis 46:27: "All the souls of the house of Jacob which came into Egypt, were threescore and ten." The word is derived from *nephesh,* a verb which appears three times in the Old Testament meaning to "revive oneself" or "refresh oneself"—again a seeming reference to life.

The late H. Wheeler Robinson, former principal of Regents Park College, wrote long ago in his excellent work *Hebrew Psychology:*

"*Nephesh* is not at all adequately rendered by 'soul.' Literary usage shows that there are three more or less distinct meanings covered by the word. . . . The first group relates to the principle of life, without any emphasis on what *we* should call its physical side, Thus the Israelite captain, threatened with destruction, says to Elijah, 'Let my *nephesh* and the *nephesh* [life] of these fifty thy servants be precious in thy sight (2 Kings 1:13).'

"Here the proper rendering is 'life,' as in the R.V., although in Jeremiah 38:16 the K.J.V. has 'as the Lord liveth, that made us this soul,' where 'life' should be rendered.

"There remains a second group of usages, the only one that can be called physical in the proper sense (though, for the Hebrew, 'physical' includes much that we should call physiological; they simply do not distinguish the two). In this group *nephesh* denotes the human consciousness in its full extent, as in Job 16:4: 'I also speak like you, if your *nephesh* were instead of my *nephesh* [soul].'

"There is no reason to doubt that the primary meaning of *nephesh* was 'breath,' like that of the Arabic, *Nafsun*—soul (*Nafasun*—breath), though there is but one instance in the Old Testament in which 'breath' is the natural rendering. It is found in Job 41:19-21.

"If then we ask the question, 'What is man?' and try to answer it, not in the old theological, but in the new physiological fashion, we shall see, that for the Hebrew, man is a unity, and that the unity in a body is a complex of parts, drawing their life and activity from breath-soul, which has no existence apart from the body.

"The Hebrews had never thought of a disembodied soul."[10] In the New Testament the equivalent is the Greek *psychē* meaning "life," "breath," or "soul." To us, of course, this Greek word has come to mean "mind" (as in *psych*ology). The mind-body problem is thus the soul-body problem. Forty times in the New Testament the King James Version translates *psychē* as "life," fifty-eight times as "soul," meaning an individual. First Peter 3:20 speaks of eight "souls" being saved in the ark of Noah. Sometimes *psychē* refers to emotions, to natural appetites or to the mind or heart.

The Hebrew word for *spirit* in the Old Testament is *ruach.* Again, there are apparently several possible meanings. Breath and wind are common. Besides translating *ruach* "spirit," the King James translators rendered the word "breath" 35 times and "wind" 117 times. Seventy-seven times the word conveys the sense of "vitality," "courage," "temper," or "anger" and refers to man's disposition. The word is also ascribed to a living principle in man and animals 25 times, seat of the emotions 3 times, and to the mind 9 times. But according to current biblical scholarship it is never seen as a conscious entity apart from the body.

The corresponding Greek word in the New Testament is *pneuma* where it is used primarily to indicate air in motion—wind or breath. By derivation it also means the life principle, frame of mind, attitudes and disposition, the basis of man's character, and incorporeal beings such as angels or demons. It is also used in reference to the Holy Spirit. But again as in *ruach* it never is used to suggest an entity in man existing apart from his body.

It is true that there are problem areas in the New Testament where the Platonic point of view seems to have conditioned the language. What, for example, did Paul mean when he speaks of being "out of the body" (2 Corinthians 12:2) and of being "absent from the body . . . to be present with the Lord?" (2 Corinthians 5:8.) Is he here inconsistent with his frequent references to the resurrection, including being called out of sleep at the coming of the Lord? (1 Thessalonians 4:13-17).

Or consider his statement: "Behold, I shew you a mystery; We shall not all sleep, but we shall all be changed, in a moment, in the twinkling of an eye, at the last trump: for the trumpet shall sound, and the dead shall be raised incorruptible, and we shall be changed. . . . When this corruptible shall have put on incorruption and this mortal shall have put on immortality, then shall be brought to pass the saying that is written, Death is swallowed up in victory." 1 Corinthians 15:51-54. (The last trump here apparently refers to the coming of the Lord referred to in 1 Thessalonians 4:13-17.)

Could Paul's question in 2 Corinthians 12:2 have to do with whether his glimpse of heaven was an inner, mystical vision or was seen with his literal eyes? And could the body he thought of being absent from in order to be with the Lord refer to *this mortal flesh* which looked forward to change?

That Hellenic influences had been at work in the thinking (or at least the language) of Jews prior to Paul's writing is well documented. Bruce Metzger of Princeton notes this, for example, in the apocryphal literature of the intertestamental period. In the Wisdom of Solomon, composed sometime between 100 B.C. and A.D. 40, we read, "The souls of the righteous are in the hand of God, and no torment will ever touch them. In the eyes of the foolish they seem to have died, and their departure was thought to be an affliction, and their going from us to be their destruction; but they are at peace. For though in the sight of men they were punished, their hope was full of immortality. Having been disciplined a little, they will receive great good, because God tested them and found them worthy of himself." Wisdom of Solomon 3:1-5.

Concerning this passage Bruce Metzger comments, "It is obvious here that Platonic ideas of inherent immortality of the soul have supplanted the Hebraic [and Christian] doctrine of the resurrection of the body, a doctrine found in Daniel 12:2 and throughout the New Testament." The basis for a later doctrine of interim purgatory is also hinted at in this passage. Of another passage in the Wisdom of Solomon, "for a perishable body weighs down the soul, and this earthly tent burdens the thoughtful mind" (Wisdom of Solomon 9:15), Metzger says, "As for man, his body is regarded as a mere weight and clog to the soul . . . , a view which is foreign to both Old Testament and New alike."[11]

By the time of Christ and shortly thereafter, the Platonic notion had apparently infiltrated Judaism to a considerable extent. Listen to Harry A. Wolfson of Harvard, who writes of "a village about thirty miles from the place of the crucifiction and only about a half century after its occurrence. We are told that when Rabban Johanan, the son of Zakkai, fell ill and was about to die, his disciples came to visit him. Upon seeing them, he began to weep. His disciples said to him: 'Light of Israel, right pillar, mighty hammer, wherefore weepest thou?' In his answer he explained that he wept because *his soul, which would survive his body,* would have to face the inscrutable judgment of the supreme King of Kings, the Holy One, blessed is He."[12]

The contrast between the Platonic Greek and the Hebraic, and thus biblical, view of man is clearly drawn in John A. T. Robinson's little monograph, *The Body, a Study in Pauline Theology*. He writes, "However much Paul may have drawn on Hellenistic sources for other parts of his doctrine, he is at any rate in his anthropology fundamentally what he describes himself, a Hebrew of the Hebrews."

After considering at some length the original words involved, John A. T. Robinson notes: "It follows from this that the third and perhaps most far reaching of all the Greek antitheses, that between *body* and *soul,* is also foreign to the Hebrew. The Hellenic conception of man has been described as that of an angel in a slot machine, as soul (the invisible, spiritual, essential ego) incarcerated in a frame of matter, from which it trusts eventually to be liberated. The body is non-essential to the personality: it is something which a man possesses, or, rather, is possessed by. 'The Hebrew idea of the personality,' on the other hand, wrote the late Dr. Wheeler Robinson in a sentence which has become famous, 'is an animated body, and not an incarnated soul' (*The People and the Book,* p. 362). Man does not *have* a body, he *is* a body. He is flesh-animated-by-soul, the whole conceived as a psycho-physical unity: . . . There is no suggestion that the soul is the essential personality, or that the soul (*nephesh*) is immortal, while the flesh (*basar*) is mortal. The soul does not survive a man—it simply goes out, draining away with the blood."[13]

Paul Tillich expressed this modern recovery of the biblical point of view when in an address to the New York Society for Clinical Psychiatry on January 14, 1960, on "The Meaning of Health"[14] he said, "Man should not be considered as a composite of several levels, such as body, soul, spirit, but as multidimensional unity. . . . In every dimension of life, all dimensions are potentially or actually present. . . . He is a unity which unites all dimensions. This doctrine stands against the dualistic theory which sees man as composed of soul and body; or body and mind; or body, soul, and spirit, etc. Man is one, uniting within himself all dimensions of life—an insight which we partly owe to the recent developments of medicine, especially psychiatry."

In a devastating conclusion, Professor Oscar Cullman says, "The answer to the question, immortality of the soul or resurrection of the dead in the New Testament, is unequivocal. The *teaching* of the great philosophers Socrates and Plato can in no way be brought into consonance with that of the New Testament."[15]

Numerous additional examples could be given. It is surprising that the idea was so long hidden—and yet not given the continuities of human thought. New ways of looking at things are extremely hard to come by for most of us.

What is not surprising is that this rebirth of a long-buried biblical way of thinking did not take place without some wrenching labor pains. Oscar Cullman, professor of the theological faculty of the University of Basel and of the Sorbonne in Paris, in his Ingersoll lecture on the immortality of man which he delivered in Andover chapel at Harvard University in April of 1955, describes the reaction he received to his presentations on the subject:

"No other publication of mine has provoked such enthusiasm or such violent hostility. The editors of the periodicals concerned have been good enough to send me some of the letters of protest which they have received from their readers. One of the letter-writers was prompted by my article to reflect bitterly that 'the French people, dying for lack of the Bread of Life, have been offered instead of bread, stones, if not serpents.' Another writer takes me for a kind of monster who delights in causing spiritual distress. 'Has M. Cullman,' he writes, 'a stone instead of a heart?' For a third, my study has been 'the cause of astonishment, sorrow and deep distress.' . . .

"My critics belong to the most varied camps. The contrast, which out of concern for the truth I have found it necessary to draw between the courageous and joyful primitive Christian hope of the resurrection of the dead and the serene philosophic expectation of the survival of the immortal soul, has displeased not only many sincere Christians in all communions and of all theological outlooks, but also those whose convictions, while not outwardly alienated from Christianity, are more strongly moulded by philosophical considerations. So far, no critic of either kind has attempted to refute me by exegesis. . . .

"This remarkable agreement seems to me to show how widespread is the mistake of attributing to primitive Christianity the Greek belief in the immortality of the soul. Further, people with such different attitudes as those I have mentioned are united in a common inability to *listen* with complete objectivity to what the texts teach us about the faith and hope of primitive Christianity, without mixing their own opinions and views that are so dear to them with their interpretation of the texts. This inability to listen is equally surprising on the part of intelligent people commited to the principles of sound, scientific exegesis and on the part of believers who profess to rely on the revelation in Holy Scripture.

"The attacks provoked by my work would impress me more if they were based on exegetical arguments. Instead I am attacked with very general considerations of a philosophical, psychological, and above all sentimental kind. [And now presumably with collections of hallucinatory anecdotes.] It has been said against me, 'I can accept the immortality of the soul, but not the resurrection of the body,' or 'I cannot believe that our loved ones merely sleep for an indeterminate period, and that I myself when I die, shall merely sleep while awaiting the resurrection. . . .'

"We must first listen to what Plato and St. Paul said. . . . We can respect and indeed admire both views. . . . But there is no reason for denying a radical difference between the Christian expectation of the resurrection of the dead and the Greek belief in the immortality of the soul. However sincere our admiration for both views, it cannot allow us to pretend, against our profound conviction and against the exegetical evidence, that they are compatible. . . .

"The fact that later Christianity effected a link between the two beliefs and that today the ordinary Christian simply confuses them has not persuaded me to be silent about what I, in common with most exegetes, regard as true; and all the more so, since the link established between the expectation of the 'resurrection of the dead' and the belief in 'the immortality of the soul' is not in fact a link at all but renunciation of one in favor of the other. 1 Corinthians 15 has been sacrificed for *Phaedo*. . . .We must recognize loyally that precisely those things which distinguish the Christian teaching from the Greek belief are at the heart of primitive Christianity."[16]

Dr. Cullman's book presents one of the clearest expressions of the New Testament's perspective and its contrast with Platonism. And, of course, this is now well known to most contemporary biblical scholars and theologians. This is not to say that they all personally subscribe to the New Testament view. And it is clearly not to say that it is a view taken or even understood by everyone at the level of the local parish. It *is* to say, however, that to those who accept the Bible as normative, near-death experiences are hallucinations. They bear little relation to an afterlife reality.

But a larger question looms over all of this. So what? Does it really make a difference whether one chooses to believe that these experiences are glimpses of something real or are merely illusions? Does one's belief about the life hereafter make any difference to this life? It is said that one day nearly 2500 years ago a disciple of Confucius asked the master, "Great teacher, tell us about life after death." Confucius replied, "We have not yet learned to know life. How can we know death?"

Let us take a look at that looming question. It may be that it is not possible to separate one's beliefs from one's actions and to put them into airtight compartments. If the history of man reveals anything at all, it seems to tell us that beliefs *do* make a difference.

References

1. Elisabeth Kübler-Ross, "Death Does Not Exist," *The Journal of Holistic Health,* 1977, p. 63.

2. See Werner Jaeger, "The Greek Ideas of Immortality," The Ingersoll Lecture for 1958, in *Immortality and Resurrection,* ed. Krister Stendahl (New York: The Macmillan Co., 1965), p. 103.

3. *Ibid.*, p. 108. Werner Jaeger speaks of Plato's Socratic dialogues as virtually the birth of a new religion.

4. Plato, *Phaedo, Five Great Dialogues* (New York: Walter J. Black, 1942), pp. 112ff.

5. *Ibid.*, pp. 145, 146.

6. *Ibid.*, p. 150.

7. See Werner Jaeger, *Phaedo,* p. 112.

8. Harry A. Wolfson, "Immortality and Resurrection in the Philosophy of the Church Fathers," *Immortality and Resurrection,* ed. Krister Stendahl (New York: The Macmillan Co., 1965), p. 57.

9. Werner Jaeger, *Phaedo,* p. 112.

10. Quoted in *Seventh-day Adventists Answer Questions on Doctrine* (Washington, D.C.: Review and Herald Publishing Association, 1957), pp. 514, 515.

11. Bruce M. Metzger, *An Introduction to the Apocrypha* (New York: Oxford University Press, 1957), pp. 74, 75.

12. Harry A. Wolfson, "Immortality and Resurrection in the Philosophy of the Church Fathers," p. 55. (Emphasis supplied.)

13. John A. T. Robinson, *The Body, A Study in Pauline Theology* (Chicago: Alec R. Allenson, Inc., 1955), p. 14.

14. Reprinted in *Perspectives in Biology and Medicine,* Autumn, 1961.

15. Oscar Cullman, *Immortality of the Soul or Resurrection of the Dead? The Witness of the New Testament* (New York: The Macmillan Co., 1964), p. 60.

16. *Ibid.*, pp. 5-8.

Prison House or Temple?

In 1948 Richard M. Weaver wrote a book (characterized by Reinold Niebuhr as "a profound diagnosis of the sickness of our culture") bearing the provocative title *Ideas Have Consequences.*[1] Ideas *do* have consequences. Ideas result in behavior. But behavior may also cause ideas or belief patterns to develop. It goes both ways.

With this chapter we shall begin to explore what were, and are, some of the consequences of a dualistic way of viewing reality. At no time before the present has mankind been more concerned with health and more informed as to the causes and cure of disease. Disregarding for the moment the "death-denial" implications of this fact, this health consciousness affords one of the most striking consequences of the rediscovery of the biblical point of view. Man is an intimate interaction and interdependency of psychic-and-somatic (mind-and-body) qualities.

In referring to man as a "multidimensional unity," Professor Paul Tillich said, "As confirmation of this idea, one may refer to psycho-somatic medicine. But although this is not incorrect, one should not forget that a hyphen between 'psycho' and 'somatic' represents the statement of a problem and not a solution.

"The multidimensional unity of life in man calls for a multidimensional concept of health, of disease, and of healing, but in such a way that it becomes obvious that in each dimension all the others are present."[2]

This notion, known as wholism (or holism), is now widely accepted in the world of medicine and elsewhere.[3] The essence of wholism is that whatever happens to a person in one aspect of his life—the psychic, physiologic, sociologic, or whatever—happens in some way to the whole of him. Healing that does not take this fact into consideration can never be more than partial and incomplete. What happens to the man's physical organism affects his mental and social well-being and vice versa.

Ellen White suggested that this also includes his moral well-being. "Whatever injures the health, not only lessens physical vigor, but tends to weaken the mental and moral powers."[4] Jesus may have had something not unlike this in mind when He said to one of His patients, "Whether it is easier, to say, Thy sins be forgiven thee; or to say, Rise up and walk?" Luke 5:23.

The wholistic (or holistic) way of thinking is affecting the practice of medicine in a variety of ways, and numerous medical authorities attest to its validity in all areas of disease and healing, including organic as well as functional disorders. Serious consideration is currently being given, for example, to psychic factors in the etiology of such diseases as cancer. On this basis, it is with interest that one observes the irony of the inclusion of the previously quoted passage by Elisabeth Kübler-Ross ("Death Does Not Exist") in *The Journal of Holistic Health*. Wholism is rooted in Hebraic soil—not in Platonic dualism. Dr. Kübler-Ross's presuppositions are inconsonant with those of the wholistic conception of man.

But let us back up a bit. Among the immediate consequences of the Neoplatonizing of Christianity as that related to the devaluing of the body were what Jacques Lacarriere called that "marvellous madness,"[5] which drove literally thousands of men and a few women into the deserts and wild places of Egypt and Syria in the early centuries of our era. There, by almost unimaginable deprivations and bodily denials, they suppressed their fleshly lusts in order to achieve spiritual excellence.

The ethos of the period was captured in St. Hildegard's statement: "God rarely dwells in a healthy body." Joseph

Goldbrunner writes of this ascetic monasticism in terms of the strivings of spirit "tugging impatiently at the chains which hamper and bind it to the earth." Goldbrunner says further, "From the first violent eruption of the monastic movement, through the Middle Ages to our own time, the tension between body and spirit remains a constant theme. . . . War is declared on the body. The dualism is present in all degrees from open hostility to latent suspicion. Asceticism is a constant wrestling with the body, a suppression of all the dangerous forces of nature, a fight against everything that pertains to the senses."[6]

Goldbrunner quotes from Francis Thompson's essay on "Health and Holiness" where he speaks of monasticism's "tyranny of the spirit over the body," of the "blind tyranny of the spirit against all flesh" as a "murderous struggle." "To drive a donkey to death was regarded as cruel, but to do the same to one's own body was thought to be meritorious."[7]

One of Lacarriere's desert ascetics, St. Dorotheus, used to choose "the greatest heat of the noonday sun for gathering stones in the desert and building cells for those who could not build them. He made one in this way every year. And when I asked him: 'What can you be thinking of, father, in your old age, to kill your body in this way in such intolerable heat?' he answered, 'I mean to kill it, since it is killing me.' "[8]

Goldbrunner notes that "before their death some of the most zealous of the saints confessed to pangs of conscience at their tyrannical treatment of their 'curse-laden bodies.' 'I was too hard on Brother Ass,' St. Francis confessed when it was too late, and it was only then that he invented the beautiful phrase 'Brother Body.' " Goldbrunner remarks, "It follows that the dualism between spirit and body must be replaced by a synthesis, if the ill-treated body is not to avenge itself and make body and soul alike diseased."[9]

He was right and St. Hildegard was wrong. God *most* dwells rather than "rarely dwells" in a healthy body! And this is what a wholistic conception of man proclaims.

Such extreme expressions of dualism are, of course, the exception in a time when it is extraordinary for persons to respond in extreme ways to any of their beliefs, particularly if it would make them uncomfortable to do so. But the implications are still there. Until recently, health consciousness and care of the body has been left to physical-culture faddists and the like or to athletes whose ends were competitive ego goals only secondarily related to good health. For most people physical health has had little to do with their "souls."

As a consequence it is one of the ironies of our more enlightened times that never have we known more about man-caused diseases, and yet never have we been more impotent in being able to do much about them—the ravages of alcohol, drugs, obesity, and tobacco to name a few. For example, after years of certainty about the relation between cigarette smoking and pulmonary and cardiovascular diseases, the total, national consumption of cigarettes has scarcely changed (although admittedly usage within the population has shifted somewhat). The ambiguity extends even into the centers of national policy. Witness the strange national schizophrenia that allows one government agency to wage propaganda war against tobacco on the one hand and another agency to subsidize the tobacco industry on the other.

The point is that we know what to do about these problems but, again, as in the case of environmental concern, how does one teach people to care? Again the most powerful motivation one might use is a wholistic one. God dwells on both floors! If "the pulse beats and breath follows breath," because "in God we live and move and have our being" and if "every breath, every throb of the heart, is a continual evidence of the power of an ever-present God,"[10] the body makes a difference! It is God's body as surely as the sky, the streams, and forests are His. If the *Earth Is the Lord's,* as Abraham Heschel suggested in the title of one of his provocative books, that term *earth* also includes man's body. Man's body was a part of that creation that was pronounced "very good," and it is to be appreciated and celebrated—dressed and kept.

It is an affront to God willfully to neglect or insult the physical organism. Might we even say a sin? It is not a sin to be sick, of course. Man is clearly not responsible for everything that happens to him in a world that is far from ideal. But it *is* sin against one's body and one's Creator to be sicker than one has to be!

Any physician who has put forth the effort has encountered the difficulty of trying to move people to control their alcohol, tobacco, and food "addictions." How does one motivate one's patients to comply with good health instructions? A discovery of the high value God places on His creation might help—at least for some—for that too is an idea with consequences.

A group of students and teachers from a western medical school were making an exploratory trek into the mountains of southern Mexico visiting and studying relatively primitive Indian groups and their health problems. They discovered that local health officials were experiencing minimal success in changing the dietary and hygiene patterns of the local Indians whose response was usually something like this: "Why should we change? Our fathers have always lived like this." And so dietary deficiency diseases, parasitosis, and other health problems continued largely unchecked.

The group came one day upon a small village that had been Christianized by a missionary body with a strong wholistic interest in health. The contrast was profound. The response was not, "Our fathers did so and so," but, "Teach us." The sanction provided by the belief that *God cared* about their bodies made all the difference. This difference was readily observable in the health of the inhabitants of that village. The story could be repeated in many parts of the world. In perhaps a more sophisticated way, it might make a difference in less primitive parts of the world as well.

That dualistic notion has made an impact also on the profession of medicine. It was not unusual in Christian circles for attention to be drawn to the fact that Greek influences were important in the early development of medicine. Its ethics, for example, is traced to one Hippocrates. But medicine really owes more to Jesus than many realize. Certainly this is true in its wholistic concept.

The association of preaching, teaching, and healing in the life and ministry of Jesus is not, to be sure, unique to Him. In widely varying primitive cultures its equivalent is found in the fact that the shaman or witch doctor is also the religious leader or priest. There is a logical base for this association. In a prescientific world, where "gods" or "spirits" often fill in the multiple informational gaps that exist, the shaman presumes to wield the magical powers of control. Ignorance about disease is one of the frightening informational gaps.

Malinowski in his study of the Trobriand people in New Guinea observed an interesting relation which became the basis for an anthropological theory. He noted that when the islanders fished in relative safety, say, in a protected lagoon, virtually no religious ritual was connected with the activity. But when they left such security for the open ocean where there was peril from storms, sharks, and hidden reefs, these forays were often accompanied by elaborate rituals.

Malinowski reasoned that the basis for this was that the anxiety that accompanied this latter kind of fishing was largely derived from its contingent, unexpected, unknown qualities. Most anxiety states derive from an element of uncertainty. By placing the unknown, and thus anxiety-producing, experience within a familiar frame of reference, the islanders had robbed the situation of its disturbing potential. (Every physician has observed something of this in the relief that is experienced by patients when labels are placed on their ailments or when familiar clinical routines are followed.) Among the Trobriands, the shaman was the one figure who could bring a measure of societal "control" to the situation.

For Jesus, by contrast, the association was not derived from magic but from His Hebraic (wholistic) background where reality knows no gulf between the psychic and the physical.

Following the lead of its founding figure, the Christian church continued to claim healing as one of its central concerns. The Acts of the Apostles and the patristic literature indicate that the practice of healing formed a major part of the regular activity of the early Church. Justin Martyr (A.D. 100-165), Irenaeus (A.D. 120-202), Tertullian (A.D. 155-230), Origen of Alexandria (A.D. 185-253), and others all demonstrate the active presence of the healing ministry in the post-apostolic church.

As late as the fourth century the Seventeenth Canon of Hippolytus contained this prayer which was ordered to be said at the ordination of bishops: "Grant him, O Lord, to loose all bonds of the iniquity of demons, the power to heal all diseases and quickly to beat down Satan under his feet."

What this prayer does not reveal, however, was the very real tension that had been developing between the church and the medical science of the day over what was seen by the church as an invasion of its prerogatives. Leslie Weatherhead points this out: "Tatian made a protest against the invasion of science. He regarded it as 'not becoming to *ascribe to matter* [italics mine] the relief of the sick,' and he asserted . . . that confidence in drugs and material remedies detracted from 'the pious acknowledgement of God.' Men did not behold God working *through* the new methods. God was left out. The drugs acted whether or not the patient believed in God. The insidious disease of materialistic humanism set in. Man has discovered drugs! He can do without God."[11]

Christian Emperor Justianian the First eventually closed down the medical schools at Athens and Alexandria because of the materialistic, and therefore "pagan," healing practices and refused further subsidies for state physicians and endowed scholars. A succession of papal edicts in the eleventh, twelfth, and thirteenth centuries forbade the study and practice of medicine and surgery by the clergy. The reason: Accepting or rendering medical treatment was widely considered to imply a lack of faith.

The medieval church's attitude toward medical science was not wholly negative, to be sure. European monasteries, where the spiritually inclined could escape from the materialistic world, actually preserved a fair amount of medical knowledge from the past. But in general, throughout much of Christian history the healing arts, considered as preoccupation with men's bodies, were relegated to an inferior status. Karl Holl's "History of the Concept 'Vocation' (Beruf)" calls attention to this in his reference to Berthold of Regensburg's dividing of the social order in the late Middle Ages into ten "choirs." At the top stood three ruling choirs: the pope with the priests; then the spiritual people, e.g. the monks; in the third place, secular magistrates, lords, and knights. Beneath these came six lower choirs,[11] from the garment maker down to the ninth—*those who dealt with medicine*. The only lower order, a tenth choir, was made up of those engaged in occupations in which doing right was thought to be impossible: prostitutes, usurers, hucksters, junk dealers, indulgence preachers, and the like.[12]

As an interesting sideline to all of this, those Roman baths, so universal a feature of Roman culture wherever it establishes itself, disappeared in Christendom long before they disappeared in Islam. The Christians repressed them not primarily because they were places of immoral behavior, which they sometimes were, but because they represented an undue pampering of the body! Islam, never having been seriously Platonized, or rather Neoplatonized, had no such reservations about the body, as anyone familiar with Koranic conceptions of heaven well knows.

In the modern period, up until the present century, some of this tension has persisted. For example, medical missionaries sent out by Protestant Christian missionary societies in the mid-1800s were considered to be little more than assistants to the "real" missionaries, the preachers and evangelists. The instructions given to a medical recruit about to leave for the west coast of Africa, in 1840, were explicit: "You are not, strictly speaking, a missionary. Your proper place is not to preach the Gospel, but to direct the energies of your mind and bring to bear your medical experience and skill in endeavoring to alleviate or to prevent the ravages of disease."[13] The medical missionary was considered as a lay member of the staff—a view widely held by Roman Catholic missions until well into this century. An American Roman Catholic writer in a review of *Catholic Medical Missions* stated in 1925, "Strange to say, the truth that man needs assistance in mind and body as well as in soul seems to have been more clearly brought out in practice in Protestant missions than our own. Among them the medical missionary is given a place of prominence; with us he has hitherto been a negligible quantity."[14]

It is of more than passing interest that a wholistic notion of healing coincided with the largely twentieth-century rediscovery of the Hebraic view of man in the Scriptures. That the two developments occurred simultaneously may not be merely coincidental. Even among Protestants the notion of wholistic healing developed slowly, about as slowly as the rediscovery of the Hebraic perspective. In 1885 the medical policy statement of a Protestant missionary society noted that medical missions were "simply as a means to an end; a helpful adjunct to the primary work of Christian evangelism. In so far as medical and surgical skill, by overcoming opposition and prejudice, could win a hearing for the Gospel, its use was to be commended."[15] But, the report reminded the recruit, it should always be remembered that "the medical work should always be subordinate to the spiritual."[16]

But by 1939 the same body was saying, "No presentation of the Gospel is complete unless it includes the care of the body and the enlightening of the mind, for only thus will that new value to human life be given to humanity which came into the world through the incarnation."[17] In 1948 the report was headed *The Health of the Whole Man.*[18] And now, of course all of this is an old tune, and a great number of voices are joining the chorus.

This is not to say, however, that every Christian physician has caught the sense of vocation that underlies that conviction. Far too many of them prefer a hyphen between Christian and physician reminiscent of what Tillich said about that hyphen between psyche and soma being "the statement of a problem and not a solution." Too few of them are ready to incorporate into their self-view what one of the founding figures in the new wholistic consciousness wrote nearly 100 years ago:

"God desires that his workers in every line shall look to Him as the Giver of all they possess. All right inventions and improvements have their source in Him who is wonderful in counsel and excellent in working. The skillful touch of the physician's hand, his power over nerve and muscle, his knowledge of the delicate organism of the body, is the wisdom of divine power, to be used in behalf of the suffering. The skill with which the carpenter uses the hammer, the strength with which the blacksmith makes the anvil ring, comes from God. He has entrusted men with talents, and He expects them to look to Him for counsel. Whatever we do, in whatever department of the work we are placed, He desires to control our minds that we may do perfect work.

"Religion and business are not two separate things; they are one. . . . Divine and human agencies are to combine in temporal as well as in spiritual achievements. They are to be united in all human pursuits, in mechanical and agricultural labors, in mercantile and scientific enterprises."[19]

Because God dwells on both floors, there is an underlying unity in all things! And thus there is an underlying sacredness in all things! There are no intrinsically sacred or profane professions or vocations—provided they are related to the divine creation. There are only sacred or profane men and women in them. The laboratory can be as holy as the chancel; the marketplace as sacred as the sanctuary. There is a holiness in doing housework, raising children, constructing a fine piece of furniture or a house, managing a business, and guiding a scalpel. As Thomas Chalmers once said, "If it be the characteristic of a worldly man that he desecrates what is holy, it should be of the Christian to consecrate what is secular and to recognize a present and presiding divinity in all things."[20]

Once there was a little saint, who had lived a long and happy life. One day God's angel came to the little saint, who was in the monastery kitchen washing pots and pans. "God has sent me," said the angel. "The time has come for you to take up your abode in eternity."

"I thank God for thinking of me," said the little saint. "But as you can see, there is this great heap of pots and pans to be washed. I don't want to seem ungrateful, but do you think I might put off taking up my abode in eternity until I have finished?"

The angel looked at him in the wise and loving way of angels. "I'll see what can be done," he said, and vanished.

The little saint went on with his pots and pans, and a great number of other things too. One day, as he stood hoeing in the garden, there again was the angel. The saint pointed with his hoe up and down the garden rows. "Look at all these weeds," he said. "Do you think eternity can hold off a little longer?" The angel smiled, and again he vanished.

The saint finished the hoeing, and then he painted the barn. What with one thing and another, time raced on until one day he was in the hospital tending the sick. He had just given a drink of cold water to a feverish patient when he looked up and there was the angel.

This time the saint just spread his hands in a gesture of resignation and compassion and drew the angel's eyes after his around the ward where all the sufferers were. Without a word the angel vanished.

That evening, when the little saint retired to his cell in the monastery and sank down on his pallet, he began to think about the angel, and how he had put him off for such a long time. Suddenly he felt very old and tired, and he said, "God, if you would like to send your angel again, I think I would like to see him now." He had no sooner spoken than the angel stood beside him. "If you still want to take me," said the saint, "I am ready now to take up my abode in eternity." The angel looked at the little saint in the wise and loving way of angels, and said, "Where do you think you have been?"[21]

That pioneer of wholism from whom we quoted earlier, E. G. White, once wrote in a similar vein, "As through Jesus we enter into rest, heaven begins here. We respond to His invitation, Come, learn of Me, and in thus coming we begin the life eternal."[22]

Certain consequences follow such thinking. Man's social institutions and structures also come to reflect his notions of reality. It was an easy step from thinking of the universe in dual categories of spirit and matter where matter plays at first a nonessential role and later a distinctly inferior one, to drawing value distinctions between the roles of men as they identified either with the material or with the spiritual realm.

Something of this came through in Berthold of Regensburg's "choirs." The spirituals, a term still current today, obviously shared in the relative value superiority granted to the realm of their commitments. And since they were able to jockey that superiority into a position of power advantage, it was only a short step to the development of a corresponding dualism of elite clergy vs. laity. The antinomy, clergy-laity that has divided the Christian church through much of its checkered history, was that consequent. This is particularly evident in any church organizational structure in which the laity counts for little.

Wholism, on the other hand, with its multidimensional unity concept, if taken seriously, possesses the power to shape a quite different kind of structure—one based not so much on relative "value" but on function and competence. Structure may still result, may indeed be necessary, but the participation of the whole is ensured—each dimension contributes in its own special way.

Paul suggests a model (significantly in the wholistic setting of the Bible) where there are many gifts, many members of the body with only one head—Christ. (See 1 Corinthians 12.) In this body each member is true to himself, to his own gifts. He does not envy another's gift or feel inferior about his own—because there is no value difference—only a difference in function. It is a body that is a multidimensional unity—a whole.

It is also, unfortunately, a model that because of human weakness is rare. The quest for power and the ubiquitous urge to dominate and exploit one's fellow men still prevails.

References

1. Chicago: University of Chicago Press.

2. See Autumn, 1961 issue of *Perspectives in Biology and Medicine.*

3. *W*holism may be the preferred rendering in the present context. *H*olism is becoming identified with an ecclectic drawing together of a wide variety of different types of therapy, including some seriously questioned by the scientific medical community.

4. E. G. White, *The Ministry of Healing* (Mountain View, Calif.: Pacific Press Publishing Association, 1905), p. 128.

5. Jacques Lacarriere, *Men Possessed by God* (Garden City, N.Y.: Doubleday & Company, 1964).

6. Joseph Goldbrunner, *Holiness Is Wholeness* (New York: Pantheon, American Book-Stratford Press, 1955), p. 19.

7. *Ibid.*, p. 20.

8. Lacarrier, *Men Possessed by God,* p. 116.

9. Goldbrunner, *Holiness Is Wholeness,* p. 21.

10. E. G. White, *Testimonies* (Mountain View, Calif.: Pacific Press Publishing Association, 1948), vol. 8, p. 260.

11. Leslie Weatherhead, *Psychology, Religion and Healing* (New York: Abingdon Press, 1951), p. 81

12. Karl Holl, "History of the Concept 'Vocation' (Beruf)," trans. H. F. Peacock (Unpublished), pp. 16, 17. (Emphasis supplied.)

13. Phyllis L. Garlick, *Man's Search for Health* (London: The Highway Press, 1952), pp. 232, 233.

14. *Ibid.*, p. 233.

15. *Ibid.*, p. 274.

16. *Ibid.*

17. *Ibid.*

18. *Ibid.*

19. E. G. White, *Christ's Object Lessons* (Washington, D.C.: Review and Herald Publishing Association), pp. 349, 350.

20. Quoted in *Mead's Encyclopedia of Religious Quotations*, p. 226.

21. James Dillet Freeman in *Daily Word*.

22. E. G. White, *The Desire of Ages* (Mountain View, Calif.: Pacific Press Publishing Association, 1898), p. 331.

In the Memory of God

Another more subtle consequence of dualistic thinking may be more fully appreciated mainly by someone conditioned to think in theological terms. That does not mean that this consequence is not important. If the concerns of theology bear any relation to reality, it may be more important than anything we have talked about thus far.

When Elisabeth Kübler-Ross entitled her article "Death Does Not Exist," she was scarcely being innovative. In principle it all had been said before. The Bible places such a pronouncement at the very beginning of things:

"Now the serpent was the sliest of all the wild creatures that God Yahweh had made. Said he to the woman [Eve] 'Even though God told you not to eat of any tree in the garden . . .' The woman interrupted the serpent, 'But we may eat of the trees in the garden! It is only about the fruit of the tree in the middle of the garden that God did say "Do not eat of it or so much as touch it, lest you die!" ' But the serpent said to the woman, 'You are not going to die. [There it is!] No, God well knows that the moment you eat of it your eyes will be opened and you will be the same as God in telling good from bad.' " Genesis 3:2-5, Anchor Bible.

Eve was referring to God's command recorded in Genesis 2:15-17 (again, the Anchor Bible rendition): "God Yahweh took the man and settled him in the garden of Eden, to till and tend it. And God Yahweh commanded the man, saying, 'You are free to eat of any tree of the garden, except only the tree of knowledge of good and bad, of which you are not to eat. For the moment you eat of it, you shall be doomed to death.' "

A strange and in some ways unsettling story. Some of our spiritual ancestors, inclined to take their Bibles literally, had trouble with this story. As literal history the account seemed simply incredible. Consequently they loaded it with a variety of allegorical nuances. Most knew who the serpent represented, of course. The Bible elsewhere had made that plain: "that old serpent, called the Devil, and Satan, which deceiveth the whole world." Revelation 12:9.

At least one later commentator, Adam Clarke, wanted to translate the Hebrew word *nachash* (in Genesis rendered "serpent") into "ape." He achieved this by ingeniously drawing on similar words in Arabic. Clarke believed that an ape would fill the bill of the story in a more satisfactory way—even allowing for an element of literalism.

A host of Bible students from Origen to modern Mormons have tried to make something of the word *knowledge* as in the King James Version is "tree of *knowledge* of good and evil." The words, "Adam *knew* his wife; and she conceived, and bare Cain" were suggestive. Even today we use the expression "carnal knowledge." These scholars' assumption was that behind the modest clothing of the Bible's poetic metaphor there was an occasion involving *sexual* awareness. (The phallic symbolism of the serpent is well known in mythology—even contemporary psychological mythology. Was this implication what Adam Clarke had in mind when he made *nachash* come out "ape"? Those kinds of stories were not unknown in our distant past.)

There were other individuals, less preoccupied with that particular brand of fantasy, who could think of "knowing" in its more usual, everyday sense. The story thus became the reinforcement of a variety of species of antiintellectualism—a posture not uncommon in religious people.

But the real thrust of the story lies deeper than such surface musings suggest. The full name of the tree in the account suggests imposed limits on a peculiar kind of knowing, not sexual, not conceptual, not propositional, but moral—the knowing of good and bad. Not that that observation helps much. Surely it is the moral sense in the man that more than any other marks him off from the beasts. The B. F. Skinners among us notwithstanding, the traditional Christian conception of man is that he is *man* precisely at the point where he chooses and thus becomes morally responsible. Everything else he shares in relative degree with his animal brothers. This power of moral choice constitutes the image of God in man.

To choose involves options or alternatives precisely like good and bad. To deny him that "tree" would be to deny man his humanness! And to give him such freedom seems to be precisely what the Creator had in mind when he brought man into existence *as man*.

Knowing good from bad seems to be a very desirable kind of knowing, does it not? If there is nothing else I can pass on to my children, at least I would hope to enable them to draw that distinction.

But perhaps the restraint had not to do with moral sensitivity but with the knowing of good and evil by firsthand experience. One does not necessarily have to learn the hard way. But that interpretation will not do either. The text attributes to God the very thing that is prohibited to man: "The moment you eat of it your eyes will be opened and you will be the *same as God* in telling good from bad." Genesis 3:5, Anchor Bible. Those were the serpent's words of course, but the thought is reinforced by God's words in verse 22: "God Yahweh said, 'Now that *man has become like one of us* in discerning good from bad, what if he should put out his hand and taste also of the tree of life and eat, and live forever!' " Anchor Bible. (Emphasis supplied.)

Now, thoughtful Christian moralists have been sure that wrong actions in man cannot be transmuted into right merely by attributing them to God. As Whittier said in his poem,

Not mine to look
Where Cherubim
  and Seraphs may not see,
But nothing can be good in Him
  which evil is in me.

No, the Scriptures we are examining must refer to something

other than the personal experience of evil because it refers to a quality in God. "Like God," the King James rendering says; and total, unmixed goodness is one of the most hallowed of all of the divine attributes.

What we seek here is a quality of experience that is good in God but is denied to man precisely because man is not God. That quality is self-sufficiency. Self-sufficiency is one of God's attributes by definition and for Him is thus good. For man self-sufficiency in any untimate sense is not so much immoral as impossible by nature. The wrong comes when man *attempts* to become self-sufficient—*attempts* to achieve what is not his to achieve. Such an attempt constitutes a rejection or denial of his creaturely status, which is what the term *sin* nearly always implies in one way or another.

Concerning this passage, Cuthbert A. Simpson writes: "The serpent in telling the woman that likeness to God is to be achieved by defiance of his command tacitly suggests that the likeness which is within human reach is likeness not in character but in power. He suggests that man can make himself the equal of God."[1]

In the story Eve eats the forbidden fruit. By this she attempts to achieve autonomy—in this instance, moral autonomy. To be morally autonomous means to derive one's norms for behavior solely from within oneself—to be a law unto oneself, to be one's own ultimate moral authority, to become "like God." God knows no law beyond or beside Himself. There is no God beyond or beside God. His law is His self-law of consistency. He is One. He alone is ultimate and unconditioned. Only God is self-existent and self-sufficient—by definition.

The ancient conundrum—"Is it right because God wills it, or does God will it because it is right?"—is an appropriate question to ask of man. It is fitting to ask whether man derives his meaning and the norms of his existence from within himself or from a reality beyond. It is nonsense, however, to ask this question of God. If He is One, is the author of all that exists, and is self-consistent, then what God wills is right by definition. Both statements are true of God simultaneously: What He wills is right because He wills it, and He wills it because it is right.

The attempt on the part of the creature to transcend creatureliness, and thus, in a sense, to reject his Creator, constitutes what Christians from time immemorial have called sin. Such an attempt represents and grows out of a distrust of God. And it demonstrates hubris—arrogant human pride.

Moral *hubris* is the most radical of all of man's attempts to be like the most high Creator. In our own time it lies behind much of what has been called "situationism." (Unfortunately, we have in much current use of this term a derogation of what was initially a useful, and in the main, a quite acceptable notion. It was originally a protest against wooden rigidity in moral conduct and insensitivity to differing circumstances. None of its creators really had in mind the freewheeling, acting-on-momentary-impulse that the term has come to imply. Joseph Fletcher, for instance, while by no means situationism's most cogent exemplar, clearly tried to steer between the Scylla of legalism and the Charybdis of antinomianism. But alas, a legion of wild spirits leaped aboard that vessel as they sought to escape from establishment morality. Now, for many, "situationism" has roughly come to mean freedom from all moral guidelines—moral autonomy—each person becoming his own measure of what constitutes good and evil. And this is precisely the point of the Garden story. Eve was tempted to deny her creaturely dependence on her Creator in the sense of "like God knowing good and bad.")

But back to the proposition "Death does not exist." In contrast to the presuppositions undergirding the "life-after-life" and the "death-does-not-exist" accounts, the Bible knows of two deaths. The first, that which "passed upon all men" is a consequence of sin. Romans 5:12. The second is the "second death," the final end of all lost sinners in a "lake of fire" at the end of time. Revelation 20:14.

The intermediate state following the first death is characterized as a "sleep." When informed of the death of his friend Lazarus, Jesus said, "Our friend Lazarus sleepeth." John 11:11. Paul wrote regarding the dead, "I would not have you ignorant, brethren, concerning them which are asleep, that ye sorrow not, even as others which have no hope," and he then elaborated this hope as the resurrection at the coming of the

Lord. 1 Thessalonians 4:13-18. In several other places as well the New Testament refers to this death as a sleep.

The Old Testament book Daniel speaks of "many of them that sleep in the dust of the earth" awakening, Daniel 12:2. This state is also characterized as one of unconsciousness. The author of Ecclesiastes wrote, "For the living know that they shall die: but the dead know not anything." Ecclesiastes 9:5. The writer of Job said, "Man that is born of a woman is of few days and full of trouble. He cometh forth like a flower, and is cut down: he fleeth also as a shadow, and continueth not. . . . Man dieth, and wasteth away: yea, man giveth up the ghost, and where is he? As the waters fail from the sea, and the flood decayeth and drieth up: so man lieth down, and riseth not: till the heavens be no more, they shall not awake, nor be raised out of their sleep. O that thou wouldest hide me in the grave, that thou wouldest keep me secret, until thy wrath be past, that thou wouldest appoint me a set time, and remember me! If a man die, shall he live again? All the days of my appointed time will I wait, till my change come. Thou shalt call, and I will answer thee." And of the state of things in the interim, he says, "His sons come to honour, and he knoweth it not: and they are brought low, but he perceiveth it not of them." Job 14:1-14, 21.

(If all this is taken at face value, a new and interesting possibility arises. In a state of total unconsciousness, there is not even an awareness of the passage of time. A friend of mine was galloping along a road on his horse. The sun was at high noon. A piece of paper, blown in the wind, startled the horse; and he jumped to one side. My friend lost his balance and fell from the horse's back. Fearful lest he be struck by the horse's hooves as he fell to the ground, he scrambled out of the way to one side. When he stood to his feet, he saw the sun hanging low over the horizon and his horse was grazing in a pasture—and he had a terrible headache! There was no awareness of the passage of the several hours he lay unconscious beside the road. His last thought before he was struck on the head by the horse's hoof merged without a break into the first thought he had upon regaining consciousness. Persons under deep anesthesia sometimes experience the same phenomenon, continuing on recovery of consciousness the sentence begun while going under anesthesia. This would mean, for our present discussion, that the call of the resurrection would be the next sound heard after one's last heartbeat—with no break between—whether you were Adam, the apostle Paul, or someone who had suffered a sudden coronary death in the twentieth century. There would be no *conscious* difference. The resurrection is thus only one heartbeat away from all of us—on the Bible's terms!)

The first death as a sleep out of which one is awakened by the resurrection is now no stranger to Bible scholars who have been able to think their way past their historically conditioned Greek concepts into the thought forms of the Hebrews who wrote the Bible. Having made this discovery, they now see quaint stories such as the one Jesus told about the rich man and Lazarus calling back and forth across the gulf fixed between heaven and hell, as just what they were meant to be, catchy parables designed to teach this-worldly lessons. They were in no way intended to contradict or modify the things Jesus said about the "sleep" and the resurrection.

The concept of the resurrection of the dead is not a comfortable one for some in our century partly because of its material overtones. "Body," even a glorified, resurrected one, tends to come under the judgment that our scientific age places upon all things physical. Since the parapsychical, like the metaphysical, tends to lie outside of material considerations and since it provides little threat to a scientific way of looking at things, presumably one could accept notions such as these and be a scientist at the same time without intellectual conflict. The concept of resurrection raises all kinds of physical questions.

The main problem for many of our contemporaries, however, derives from the loss of a belief in a Creator and a creation, for the resurrection *is* a creation, or rather a *re*-creation analogous to the Genesis account of the origin of man. It is not simply the resuscitation of a form that has suffered arrest of its vital-organ systems. It differs in some respects, thus from the biblical resurrections by Jesus, even that of Jesus Himself. His resurrection appears to be in some ways a special case. All of the accounts of Jesus' own resurrection describe an empty tomb.

His old body was missing from the tomb; and yet His resurrected body was different, in spite of the continued presence of the crucifixion nail prints and the wound in His side. In line with this, Paul writes in his long discourse on the resurrection in 1 Corinthians 15, of a resurrected body that is glorified, celestial, incorruptible, spiritual, immortal, and heavenly, whatever all of these terms mean. According to Paul, at the resurrection "in a moment, in the twinkling of an eye, at the last trump . . . *we shall be changed.*" Verses 52, 53. (Emphasis supplied.)

In some ways this might seem to render invalid what was said earlier in the discussion on wholism. If we are going to receive new bodies, who cares over much what happens to the old ones—the health question? But that's dualistic thinking. What is this "we" who are going to receive new bodies? On the Bible's terms this "we" has no independent, real existence apart from the body. (Remember, biblically, "man does not *have* a body, he *is* a body.") What one *is*, became so in a body with which it is inseparably connected.

Does this mean, then, that the very material particles which were once "me" are reintegrated, put back together again, though perhaps in a new way, with a new "celestial" quality to which Paul refers, immortal now, but still in some way what was previously there?

That would be a very complicated matter as every biologist knows. The biosphere, that part of our world where life goes on, is a complex system of interaction and interchange. All of us possess in our bodies particles, elements, atoms, and molecules that at one time functioned in the bodies of other living forms. At death these go back into the soil and atmosphere (biosphere) and are picked up in the complicated food chain and recycled perhaps innumerable times. Atoms of carbon, nitrogen, calcium, etc., are presently in the bodies of all of us that once served plants, dinosaurs, perhaps other mammals, even other humans. The fact is that even in our own organism everything is in constant flux. There is almost nothing in one's body that was there even a few years ago—except perhaps the enamel of the teeth. The elemental particles come and go, flow in and out—even from one cell to another—and cycle back into the biosphere possibly entering into the life flow of others.

A good analogy is a flowing river. A river is in constant change, at least as far as the individual molecules of water are concerned. (Heraclytus once said, "You step, and you do not step into the same river twice." The later philosopher Cratylus, who is supposed to have communicated by crooking his little finger, said when he heard Heraclytus's aphorism, "Ha, you can't even step into the same river once.") And yet one speaks of a particular river, gives it a name, and draws it in on maps. Even if it has no water in it for periods of the year, as is the case with some of the rivers of our Southwest, this is still true. When the water comes back again, it is still the same river it was last season. Even while the water is absent, we leave the signs up and the maps intact—and people remember.

But while the water flows one is able to identify things that remain relatively constant, this eddy, these rapids, that bend. Have you never stood by a rushing stream and admired a particular ripple that stood still as the water rushed by? Man's life is like that. As the stream of matter flows in and out, there is a *constancy of form;* and therefore we are able to shave and wash the right face in the morning and recognize our children and our friends.

There is a gradual change of form also, of course, as anybody knows who has finally gone back to one of those alumni meetings; but ordinarily it occurs slowly enough to allow us to adjust to it and to maintain a sense of personal identity. (If Rip Van Winkle had really slept those twenty years, looking at his face in the mirror on awakening would have really been quite unnerving.)

Who is this "I," then; who is this body? Ultimately it is a matter of form more than of substance, a continuity of form at work synthesizing the living stream of past and present existence and experience, creating, choosing, remembering.

All that my personal resurrection requires is that *this* form be recreated with its own private memories and personality characteristics. No divine artificer would have to scramble around trying to reassemble all the complex parts, the molecules, at least some of which we might be sharing with others in the biosphere. But, and this is important to the moral implications of health, remember the "form" is in some measure vulnerable to the "substance" if wholism means anything at all. "You are what you eat" may not be entirely true, but "You are what you have done" is at least as valid. And what you have done was done as a dynamic, integrated, whole—body, mind and soul.

The biblical resurrection requires, then, only two qualities, neither of which competes with the scientific outlook since each is on a different plane from science ordinarily conceived. They are, one, a Creator who can put substantial things together, and, two, a Creator who remembers *you*. The same author who penned "the dead know not any thing," also wrote "the spirit shall return unto God who gave it." Ecclesiastes 12:7. Perhaps this remembering of a specific "you" is the real sense of this interesting remark. Not only the gift of *life* returns to the giver, but in some way each precious, individual person is preserved there against the day of the resurrection—would it be appropriate to say in contemporary metaphor, "preserved in the memory banks of heaven"? God remembers and therefore we have a future—a life after this.

One of the reasons for belief in an immortal soul derives from the need for continuity. Each person who is a living, changing stream is also a continuity as he changes. (Interestingly, Plato described the soul as unchanging while the body changed.) The notion of a future with a break between, strains the sense of sameness. If I do not exist in the interim, is the resurrected me the same person who disintegrates into "dust" at death?

The message of the Bible is that I *do* exist. Even in death I exist in the mind of God like those dry Southwestern rivers exist in our minds. He provides the continuity between the now and the then. He who numbers the hairs of your head (in Jesus' metaphor) preserves (in our metaphor) the record of all that complex psycho-neurologic chemistry, the DNA and all that is associated, the memory, the personality, the character, and the behavioral peculiarities—each of which helps to constitute every precious individual person. He remembers and recreates it all at the appointed time, at the resurrection. To believe this, of course, requires a prior belief that God can create on such a scale—which is also, you will recall, a biblical notion.

In one sense such a re-creation would be more complex than the original. In the biblical model, man comes on the scene as a new creation. At the resurrection God creates anew, but the creature also is given his past with whatever modifications are appropriate. The "change" to which Paul refers as occurring at the resurrection of the redeemed involves a kind of renewal that jettisons those marks of evil that were not the true essence of the person. Some things one does, do not represent the essential person as a child of God. Perhaps the future does not burden us with such, and there is thus a *wholly "glorified" self* raised up in the resurrection. The future is also about wholeness. But that glorification is not a discontinuity.

The concept of constant change would require some selectivity on the part of God. At what stage in my life does my present correspond to my future self in God? Surely none of us would choose a future life which was continuous with the senile degenerations most people suffer before they depart *this* life.

I recall a patient who had been at his prime an honored and respected clergyman. I saw the mementos of this in his home, the pictures, his academic credentials, the honors which had been given to him. When I knew him, however, all of this was past. Senile changes had ravaged his once fine mind and personality. In my office he would mouth foul language and scatological attempts at humor causing his prim, refined preacher's wife to cringe with embarrassment. "Why does he do things like this?" she would cry in anguish. My attempts to console her, to let her know that I understood that this was senility and that he was not responsible for what he said and did, were futile.

Part of the message of the Bible regarding the resurrection and the change is that it involves a God who knows, remembers and selects the best form for the future. It means, at the very least, the continuity will represent each man at his best, not at his worst. Can this be proven? No. It follows from what the life of His Son tells us about the Father of us all. God provides the continuity, and you can trust Him.

Which brings us to the major point of this discussion about life after death.

References

1. Cuthbert A. Simpson, *The Interpreter's Bible*, vol. 1, p. 505.

Into His Hands

In the Genesis account of the fall of man, ("In the day that thou eatest thereof thou shalt surely die," KJV) the threatened death did not come as a direct consequence of the eating of the fruit, nor was it immediate. The Hebrew can be rendered like this: "For the moment you eat of it, you shall be doomed to death," Anchor Bible. The text emphasizes certainty rather than immediacy.

The fruit itself, moreover, was not the cause of death. In the story man was to die the first death by exclusion from the other tree in the garden, the tree of life. Cherubim were placed with "a flaming sword which turned every way, to keep the way of the tree of life." Genesis 3:24. Thus God Himself is depicted as withdrawing from them access to that which was required for living forever. (See Genesis 3:22.) What does all of this mean?

At least a part of what it means is this: having tasted of self-sufficiency, human beings would never again be the same. Their garden experience had not been without its symbolic reminders of their creaturely dependence on God: the tree of life, the weekly Sabbath, the tree of knowledge of good and evil with its warning. Primal man was a creature, and his limits were creaturely limits. But with the rejection of creatureliness came the hubris which separated him and his progeny from their real existence.

Man was created to be responsibly dependent on Someone greater than himself. Within his creaturely bounds he was given responsible freedom, creativity, and dominion over his world. But he was still dependent. The rejection of his dependence upon his Creator was tantamount to the rejection of the essence of his own existence. And that rejection has had consequences. The long dismal story of man can be told largely in terms of man's striving for autonomy. And almost everything evil and destructive he has done can be traced in some way to that compulsive restlessness. In contrast, almost everything good in his history has come from a return to responsible, trusting acceptance of the Creator's way for him, acceptance of himself as creature and thus acceptance of and openness to others.

Professor Tillich once spoke of three contrasting motifs: autonomy, heteronomy and theonomy. We have referred to autonomy, the compulsion to self-sufficiency. In a community autonomy must give way to heteronomy; that is, the domination of one by another, for self-sufficiency can never be absolute in a group, since interdependence is the essence of groupness and community. In cases where the individual members of a group attempt to "go it alone" community disintegrates almost by definition. When such disintegration occurs autonomy again obtains, but at the expense of heteronomy.

The third category—theonomy—alone provides the possibility of a true community of persons. Theonomy requires the responsible "resting in the hands of God." And this ends all destructive struggle for dominion one over another.

Jesus contrasted autonomy-heteronomy with theonomy when He said to His disciples, "Ye know that the princes of the Gentiles exercise dominion over them, and they that are great exercise authority upon them. But it shall not be so among you. . . . Whosoever shall be chief among you, let him be your servant." Matthew 20:25-27. These two contrasting value systems have characterized the conflict between good and evil in the world throughout most of human history.

The urge to autonomy-heteronomy is based on weakness, not on strength. It is a coping ploy for inadequacy and uncertainty. It is the cloak that unaccepted finitude wears. Creatureliness perceived as being "limited" is the ground from which the temptation to play the "unlimited" God role grows. Only the self-accepting person can also accept the way things are. I can trust myself in the hands of God and be open to my fellows only when I accept what I am. When I cannot trust God, I must try to *be* God and put down my neighbors. And it is this "sin" that passed to all men.

And so there was placed a barrier at the tree of life—as a protection against human hubris—pride. It was said in Genesis 3:17, "Cursed is the ground for thy sake." "For thy sake" could mean "because of you." But there is a sense in which "for thy sake" suggests a value to be gained. In this latter sense a bad thing may be transformed to a good purpose. And what was true of toil and sorrow may also be true of death, the "first death." They each may remind us of our finitude.

If the ultimate death, the second death, is the final outcome of rebellion and alienation from God, which are the logical corollary of self-sufficiency and independence from God, the "first death," even with its potential for human tragedy and sadness, might actually serve as a hedge against the second.

There are many little, daily relative reminders of our creaturely finitude; but death is the absolute reminder. Death is the one basic fact of human existence over which man has no absolute control. He can delay it, drag himself back from its grasp temporarily, make it more comfortable (or miserable); but ultimately every human attempt to prevent or deny it is doomed to failure. Resist it with whatever wealth, power, or technical skill one will—it is the one inevitable fact of life. And every man stands humbled in its presence; whether he is Alexander, Napoleon, Adolph Hitler, J. Paul Getty, or Howard Hughes—it's all the same. And according to the Bible's teaching there is no hope beyond—except from God.

The message of the Bible regarding the resurrection is that there *is* life after death—but *not because of something inherent in me*. It is because God remembers me and restores me to life again at His appointed time. It is also a message that if there is no God who remembers, the grave is the end. Death is the absolute reminder of my final and absolute dependence upon God for my existence.

Thus, as shattering as the first death can be, it still may be at times the better of the available options. The second death is a far greater tragedy. Could it be that God has allowed the first death to protect us from the sin that leads to the second? The first death is certainly tragic. And God may weep more than we all when it occurs, even though He knows of the certainty of the resurrection. (Isn't this the real significance of Jesus' weeping at Lazarus's tomb?) Yet it may be the ultimate protection against the consequences of the Fall in all of us. This may be a reason why the enemy of God tried to convince our first parents that death does not exist. The serpent's lie was intended to counter God's efforts to enable man to fulfill his own God-inspired potential.

Death-denial thus opposes the tree of life, the tree of knowledge of good and evil, and God's Sabbath; all these were designed to help man to be what he was created to be, a wondrous creature responsibly dependent upon God as he exercised dominion over the world. It is no coincidence that the lie appears again at the end of time as it did at its beginning.

The doctrines of the resurrection and the Sabbath are part and parcel of one truth. The Creator reigns supreme. All of His creatures ultimately derive their existence, continued sustenance, and meaning from Him, and from Him alone.

The Scriptures speak of a war at the end of time—a war against a "remnant" who place God first in complete trust. May we be witnessing the opening skirmishes in that final conflict? Never was there a time when it was more important to know what and why one believes, but above all, to know *whom* one believes. Paul in his letter to Timothy says, "I know whom I have believed and am persuaded that he is able to keep that which I've committed unto him against that day." 2 Timothy 1:12. In Paul's mind "that day" is the day of his resurrection. He is not afraid to die. Certainly he is not so afraid that he has to deny the reality of his death—because he knows God.

Raymond Moody chose *Life After Life* as the title of his book because he did not believe that his subjects were ever actually dead. He repeatedly spoke of their being "near death." But he also chose the title because his belief was similar to that of Dr. Kübler-Ross, that death does not exist. But is there life after *life*? No, not on the Bible's terms, except for those to whom Paul refers who remain alive at the time of the resurrection.

There *is* life after *death*. That's the message of the Bible—and it is so only because God remembers. There is nothing in us that guarantees it. Our life is hid in God— in the "memory banks of heaven." And we may know it, not because we have discovered some mysterious fact about ourselves, but because we accept a long-established fact that God is our Creator and Redeemer. We may know it *because of who He is* and because we with the apostle Paul know *Him*.

This opens to us another clear message of the Bible. (And this may be the most important of the whole story.) Death, in the metaphor of the Word of God, is a symbol of sin. Paul writes of "being dead in your sins" (Colossians 2:13) and uses the figure of Christian baptism—in its original sense of being totally immersed under water—to describe the Christian's transformation through death, burial, and resurrection. (See Romans 6:4-11.)

The metaphor is apt. The death denial to which the brilliant social critic Ernest Becker refers, that frenzied human struggle against the ultimate anxiety of nonbeing, can be transposed, almost without missing a beat, to a consideration of the spiritual state of fallen man.

In the Eden story as soon as Adam and Eve had eaten of the forbidden fruit, the Scripture says, "They knew that they were naked." Immediately they fashioned for themselves fig-leaf aprons to cover their barrenness—and those fig leaves have been woven into the human fabric ever since.

Death-anxiety has its counterpart in guilt-anxiety—the state of alienation from self, from others, and from God. It is experienced in a variety of ways—self-disesteem, anxiety, aloneness, meaninglessness—existential nakedness. Often it is disguised as a vague uneasiness and a restlessness—a fear of being alone, a fear of the dark. The psychodynamic origins of this anxiety are complex, but everyone knows the feeling. We all share in it one way or another, and we know it when we drop our fig leaves long enough to take a good look at ourselves.

There are coping mechanisms here as there are in death denial, and they frequently correspond. For weakness, insecurity, inferiority, and self-disesteem there are the pride-marks, the status symbols, competitive strivings, and self-assertive attempts to appear important. For guilt we assume postures of self-righteousness and moral pride, while calling all others sinners. From fear and loneliness we arrange escapes through drugs, alcohol, sensual preoccupation, and frenzied pursuits of hedonic satisfaction. From feelings of our own unworthiness we pull others down and exploit them.

But here, just as in death-denial "games," one cannot really hide from the truth. The coping mechanisms tend only to deepen the problem by creating surface illusions which drive the monstrous fear beneath the tissues where it festers and erodes life's forces.

In coping with the anxiety of death, as with the anxiety of estrangement, one usually indulges in reality denial such as creating illusions of self-sufficiency and freedom from the specter that haunts our days.

But usually the coping mechanisms compound the problem. They create a vicious cycle in which our shabby attempts to cover our existential nakedness only serve to deepen our sense of alienation and guilt-shame. What is worse, we pass the problem along to the next generation, trapping our children also in the toils of our failure.

Paul must have felt something like this when he cried out in the anguish of his soul, "O wretched man that I am! who shall deliver me from the body of this death?" Romans 7:24.

Most of our own attempts to deliver ourselves and each other from the incubus of our sinfulness are directed at breaking the wheel of our sin at the level of behavior. We punish, cajole, threaten, and reward in our effort to modify the coping, so that it might become less destructive and inconvenient. But behavior modification without getting at the root of the problem is like attempting to eliminate the crabgrass by mowing the lawn. The crabgrass takes over anyway.

The death analogy is again useful. Death-anxiety is not assuaged by surface denial. The way to deal with death is to accept courageously its incorporation into the fabric of living. The existentialists have a point here. But this is not possible without its incorporation into the *full* fabric of living, a fabric that includes the Author and Ground of our being.

Jesus' experience points the way. It is obvious from the

record that He also encountered death in its full power. Professor Cullmann in his book on immortality of the soul and the resurrection makes a point of the difference between Jesus' death-anticipation and that of Socrates. It was his thesis that the two points of view were radically different. Socrates faced death with calmness and equanimity—even almost with eagerness since for him it did not exist as a reality.

According to Cullmann, Jesus' agony in the Garden of Gethsemane was, by contrast, one in which death as nonbeing was intensely real. He experienced none of the Socratic assurance. Cullmann has a point, but it would be better applied later in the story. Gethsemane was not that simple. It could be that at that moment in His experience, what He must anticipate prior to His death was mainly what weighed on His soul—agony that could render death a welcome release. (The kind of thing cancer patients worry about.) In Jesus' dying there was nothing so simple as drinking hemlock in the comfort of one's drawing room surrounded by friends.

In any case, the point of relevance to our present discussion occurs somewhat later as He neared the end of His life on the cross. In those last moments He hangs utterly naked before the stark reality. It is a terrifying picture that stabs deep into the soul. "My God, my God, why hast thou forsaken me?" He screams to the black heavens—which offer no window of hope, no escape, no denial. He is utterly and completely vulnerable and alone. But *note what He does in His extremity*. Incredible! But He does it—He places His life totally into the hands of God. "Into thy hands."

And this is the real meaning of resurrection, of the declaration "Death is swallowed up in victory. O death, where is thy sting, O grave, where is thy victory" 1 Corinthians 15:54, 55. And there is Easter morning.

In this Jesus pointed the way. It is the only victorious way to cope with the ultimate anxiety: "Into thy hands." But in this He also indicated the way to deal with the wretchedness that is the state of fallen man. And this is the reason for discussing sin in a book on death. The two, death-anxiety and guilt-anxiety, are cut from the same bolt of cloth—as are their solutions. The way to deal with the anxiety of alienation too is to look at it squarely in the face—no evasions, no tricks, no papering over—squarely in the face, and then to *put it in God's hands*. That's what is meant by being saved by grace and not by works. It means to trust God totally for the resurrection—the new creation!

If we would only trustfully do this, how many of the destructive things we do to ourselves and to each other would cease to have any power over us. How buoyant would be our celebration of the new being in Christ Jesus.

True, because each of us has a past, we might have to place ourselves in God's hands again and again in the case of this anxiety. Paul speaks of dying daily. 1 Corinthians 15:31. But this "death" is always followed by a "resurrection"—again, again, and again—as often as needed. And may I submit, followed by a celebration of the new creation in buoyant, responsible, released living. After the Creation Adam and Eve were given the privilege of dressing and keeping the garden, and that is part of the celebration. A new, creative life!

This may be the primary justification for looking seriously at the new mood regarding dying and for reexamining the implications of a Neoplatonic, immortal soul conception verses the biblical resurrection. The corollary of death is sin, and what is true of one is true of the other. Just as there is, according to the Bible, nothing in me that guarantees the future after death, there is nothing good in me that enables me to overcome the human problem—that is, the deeper problem behind the problems. No playing games at the surface of things, no fig-leaf aprons can cover the fact that in reality I am utterly naked. Accepting that fact, incorporating it, and then surrendering my denial mechanisms into the hands of God guarantee the future.

Elisabeth Kübler-Ross concludes her article, "Death Does Not Exist," this way: "Only if you keep a very, very open channel, an open mind, and no fear, will great insight and revelations come to you. . . . You don't have to do anything except learn to get in touch in silence within yourself. . . . Get in touch with your own inner self, and learn not to be afraid. And one way not to be afraid is to know that death does not exist."[1]

One can appreciate her positive, optimistic counsel, but it is counsel misplaced. The only way to be unafraid of the future is to place one's life in the hands of Him who holds the future. The future is not in me; the future is in God. I shall live again because He lives and because He graciously remembers me.

References

1. Elisabeth Kübler-Ross, "Death Does Not Exist," *The Journal of Holistic Health,* 1977, p. 65.